the 5:2

FASTING COOKBOOK

DELICIOUS RECIPES FOR **100**, **200** AND **300** CALORIE MEALS

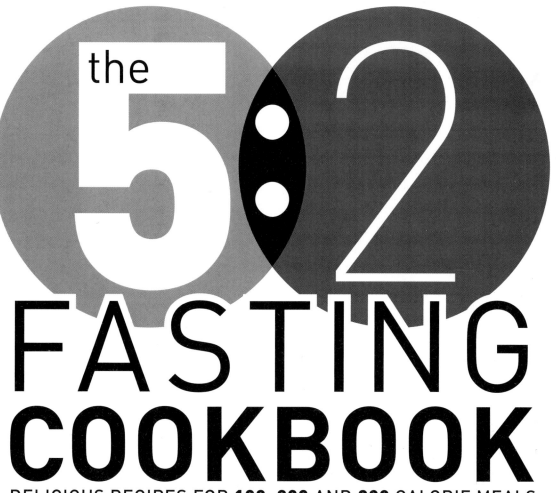

ANGELA DOWDE
NUTRITIONIST OF THE YEAR

hamlyn

Angela Dowden is a registered nutritionist who writes on diet and health for numerous newspapers and magazines. She was awarded the Nutrition and Health Writer/Broadcaster of the Year award in 2012.

An Hachette UK Company
www.hachette.co.uk
First published in Great Britain in 2013 by
Hamlyn a division of Octopus Publishing Group Ltd
Endeavour House
189 Shaftesbury Avenue
London
WC2H 8JY
www.octopusbooks.co.uk

Copyright © Octopus Publishing Group Ltd 2013

ISBN 978-0-600-62807-1

A CIP catalogue record for this book is available from the British Library

Printed and bound in Italy

1 3 5 7 9 10 8 6 4 2

Both metric and imperial measurements are given for the recipes. Use one set of measures only, not a mixture of both.

Standard level spoon measurements are used in all recipes
1 tablespoon = 15 ml
1 teaspoon = 5 ml

Ovens should be preheated to the specified temperature. If using a fan-assisted oven, follow the manufacturer's instructions for adjusting the time and temperature. Grills should also be preheated.

This book includes dishes made with nuts and nut derivatives. It is advisable for those with known allergic reactions to nuts and nut derivatives and those who may be potentially vulnerable to these allergies, such as pregnant and nursing mothers, invalids, the elderly, babies and children, to avoid dishes made with nuts and nut oils.

The Department of Health advises that eggs should not be consumed raw. This book contains some dishes made with raw or lightly cooked eggs. It is prudent for more vulnerable people such as pregnant and nursing mothers, invalids, the elderly, babies and young children to avoid uncooked or lightly cooked dishes made with eggs.

Contents

Introduction 4

What is intermittent fasting? 6

The health benefits 10

Getting started 14

Fast day eating 18

What to expect on the 5:2 diet 24

10 ways to make the 5:2 diet work for you 28

5:2 for life 32

4-week fast day meal planner 33

Give yourself a treat 36

Recipes **38**

Breakfasts 40

Lunches 50

Dinners 80

Desserts 122

Calorie counter 140

Index 143

Acknowledgements 144

Introduction

If you've picked up this book you may already be a convert to intermittent fasting. Alternatively, you may have heard about its benefits and are wondering whether to give it a go. At the other end of the scale you may be a battle-weary diet sceptic, still holding out a small hope you'll one day find the way to shape up and feel healthier permanently. Whatever your starting point or motivation, if you have a small or large amount of weight to lose and would like to feel more comfortable in your own skin, it's for you too.

So what is the 5:2 approach to weight loss and how does it work? There are any number of ways people practise intermittent fasting, from one day of light eating a week to no food at all for several days in a row. The 5:2 approach works well for most people because it's a pragmatic solution that steers a safe, doable and yet effective path through these extremes.

How to use the book

The 5:2 plan allows normal eating (including treats and meals out) for five days a week and then restricts calorie intake to 500 calories a day for women and 600 calories for men (a quarter of the normal recommended daily intake) for the other two. For most people, it's the perfect compromise that allows for socializing, family life and work commitments, while still introducing enough calorie control to make sure you lose weight at a healthy rate.

With its delicious and innovative recipe selection, this book shows just how flexibly you can consume your 500 or 600 calories to keep the hunger wolf from the door and, yes, even tickle your taste buds at the same time! It also includes some sweet treats that are suitable for a fast day.

Ultimately, you'll be losing weight by eating, overall, fewer calories than your body uses up. But where the 5:2 diet is particularly brilliant is how marvellously achievable it can make this task for food lovers. People who find success with 5:2 often report that they failed to lose weight in the past because cutting back every day was such a struggle – doing so for just a couple of days a week, albeit more drastically, is a much more attractive proposition. Better still, far from being a short-term fad, those who practise intermittent fasting find it is a lifestyle choice that they can stick to because it doesn't take over their whole life, doesn't demonize specific foods and can even run alongside other supportive weight-loss regimens, such as online food diary methods.

As to the health benefits? As you lose body fat and get trimmer, you can expect to greatly reduce your chance of having a heart attack or developing heart disease. And, in strands of research unrelated to the weight-loss benefits, there's a growing groundswell of science that shows that periodically putting your body into a fasted state may cause various chemical changes linked with lower risk of age-related diseases and higher chance of living healthier for longer.

Whether you're a 5:2 fan in search of food inspiration, or just intrigued to know more, you'll find something in this book for you. Read, digest, get slimmer and enjoy!

IS THE 5:2 DIET FOR EVERYONE?

Most overweight adults can benefit from a 5:2 diet, but it should never be embarked on by children or adolescents, for whom any form of nutritional stress is undesirable. Also, do not do the 5:2 diet if any of the following apply (check with your medical practitioner if you are uncertain).

- You are pregnant, trying to get pregnant or breastfeeding.
- You are already at the bottom end of your healthy weight. You can check this using an online Body Mass Index (BMI) calculator – a BMI of 20 or less would indicate you are not a candidate for 5:2, or indeed any weight-loss programme.
- You are an elite athlete or in training for a marathon or other big stamina event.
- You are diabetic.
- You have irritable bowel syndrome.
- You have been diagnosed with an eating disorder, either recently or in the past.

What is intermittent fasting?

People have fasted – out of choice or through necessity – for millennia, so the general concept is far from new. Interest was roused in the 1930s (and repeatedly since) when scientists found that restricting the calories fed to various animals and insects increased their lifespan. The idea of severely restricting calories every other day – rather than by a smaller amount every day – came later, in 2003, with laboratory research carried out at the National Institute on Aging (NIA) in America. The concept of intermittent fasting – and more specifically the 5:2 diet – for managing weight reached a mass audience when Dr Michael Mosley presented the theories in a BBC *Horizon* programme aired in August 2012.

Fasting is nothing new!

Fasting for physical wellbeing and spiritual reflection is as old as the hills and all of the big religions, such as Judaism, Buddhism, Christianity and Islam, embrace it. It's only in modern times that we've become obsessed by the notion that we'll grow weak and depleted if we don't graze on food around the clock. In fact, you don't have to think too long about it to realize that a menu of regularly spaced meals and snacks is probably more alien to our body than periods of feast followed by periods of famine. For cavemen and women, there would undoubtedly have been periods when they were subsisting only on berries, roots and leaves until the next animal kill, when they were able to stock up on concentrated calories ready for further lean times ahead.

Nowadays, despite being bombarded with never-ending eating opportunities, our bodies are still designed with biology and hormones that expect food to be scarce at some times and more plentiful at others. This is why many scientists believe intermittent fasting could be a particularly healthy and physiologically appropriate way to keep trim and fight ageing.

As well as suiting our biology, intermittent fasting also works well on a psychological level. The 'carrot' of being able to eat without depriving yourself for five days a week far outweighs the 'stick' of two much tougher days each week.

Addressing 5:2 diet concerns

Any 'new' diet or weight loss regimen is likely to attract critical attention, and intermittent fasting is no exception. This is especially the case given that there are any number of ways (of varying levels of sensibleness and safety) that you can do the diet, and any types of food you can include or avoid.

Suffice to say, as a registered nutritionist, I had to be completely confident that the particular version of 5:2 fasting described in these pages can do no harm. And, for the record, I am completely confident that this is so. However, to deal with some specific points that might worry you, read on.

HAVEN'T STUDIES SHOWN THAT PEOPLE FIND INTERMITTENT FASTING HARDER THAN NORMAL CALORIE COUNTING?

This worried me, too, when I read a 2011 paper by Dr Michelle Harvie and the team at Genesis Breast Cancer Prevention, a charity in Manchester. It compared obese women following a 5:2-style programme with obese women on modest calorie restriction every day, and found fewer of those in the intermittent fasting group reported that they would continue with the regimen. Dr Harvie has since modified and improved the diet, however, and in a further, more recent clinical trial, her subjects were significantly more likely to stick to the fasting regimen than normal calorie restriction. I guess this usefully illustrates the importance of finding a version of 5:2 eating that you can actually *enjoy*. Let's not pretend that any one regimen is always going to work for everyone, though – if something doesn't work for you, don't do it!

FASTING MAY BE OKAY FOR MEN, BUT ISN'T IT BAD FOR WOMEN?

The basis of this argument seems to be that women have lower lean tissue levels and as such have less reserve if skipped meals lead to the breakdown of essential muscle. Even if this were a concern – and studies of moderate intermittent fasting regimes suggest it's not – this is covered by eating modest amounts of protein on your fast day (see Fast Day Eating guidelines on page 19). Another small study that compared the experiences of eight non-obese men and women might also seem a blow to females, as it concluded that intermittent fasting seemed to 'adversely affect glucose tolerance in non-obese women but not in non-obese men'. However, the subjects were on a harsh regimen with no food at all for 36 hours in every 48-hour period. Obese women following much gentler routines, like the one advocated in this book, show very good responses in blood glucose levels and markers of diabetes risk (see page 12).

I HEARD IT COULD AFFECT FERTILITY?

As long as you eat your 500 calories on fast days you're not being too extreme and there is no evidence whatsoever that female fertility will be affected. Being very overweight is much more likely to affect your fertility, and 5:2 is an effective way to tackle being overweight. However, to be on the safe side, don't follow a 5:2 diet if you are actively trying for a baby. Being very thin will also affect fertility.

DOESN'T 'FASTING' ENCOURAGE EATING DISORDERS?

We're very clear that you shouldn't try intermittent fasting if you have ever had an eating disorder. This is just to be safe in case it unearths any old obsessive behaviours. More lengthy forms of fasting may be somewhat addictive but 5:2 isn't a food-free fast at all, it's just a restricted-calorie one. There is no evidence at all that it can trigger a new eating disorder.

HOW ABOUT BREAKFAST?

Skipping this meal is particularly frowned upon by experts, but most intermittent fasters will eat it on a fast day. However, don't force yourself to do so if you prefer not to: although breakfast eating is clearly associated with better health and weight, breakfast eaters also tend to have many other healthy habits, such as watching saturated fat intake and doing more exercise, which collectively explain the benefits.

ISN'T SKIPPING MEALS BAD FOR YOU?

If skipping meals is part of a generally erratic and unhealthy pattern of eating, where you lurch from one unhealthy snack to another in lieu of proper balanced meals, then yes. However, with the type of controlled food restriction advocated by 5:2, the focus is on getting good nutrition despite having very few calories. There's now also lots of evidence showing that, far from being bad for you, periods with no or very little food intake are actually healthy, provided, as outlined on page 5 and above, you don't have a medical or psychological condition that prohibits it.

ARE 5:2 REGIMENS STRICT ENOUGH TO GET MAXIMAL HEALTH BENEFITS?

One criticism, usually from academic quarters, is that 5:2 fasting doesn't actually deliver as many health benefits as it could and that periods of 18–36 hours without food are needed for potential protection against conditions like Alzheimer's and cancer. This is at odds with what's conventionally thought safe and sensible, so is there a sensible compromise? If you want to potentially maximize the benefits of 5:2, one way may be to try eating just one meal on your fast day, and to make it lunch or dinner (you could try two or three courses adding up to 500 or 600 calories from our recipe section). However, fasting in any prolonged fashion is beyond the remit of this book, and the focus of our 5:2 advice is safe and efficient weight loss, so never do anything that feels uncomfortable.

The health benefits

As with any emerging new science, intermittent fasting attracts a variety of expert opinion and debate, from 'evidence that intermittent fasting can have health benefits is very strong' (Professor Mark Mattson, Chief of the Laboratory of Neurosciences at the US National Institute on Aging) to 'limited evidence base for intermittent fasting in general' (our very own NHS).

What's undeniable is that the research into the health benefits of intermittent fasting is really picking up and, although to date the number of human studies may have been rather small, this is rapidly changing, with new results coming out all the time.

In fact, so much so that it's hard to keep up unless you're immersed on a daily basis in this academic area – which is probably why www.nhs.uk scattered its review of 5:2 dieting with caveats warning readers it was an 'unsystematic review' and 'not an exhaustive "last word" on the topic'. Suffice to say, the top researchers in the area of intermittent fasting – most of them at American universities – tend to get a lot more excited and evangelical than serious academics normally have a wont to do when it comes to their particular areas of research. Many practise intermittent fasting themselves – and often hardcore versions – because they are so convinced of the benefits.

So what do we know are the benefits of intermittent fasting so far?

Weight loss

When you only eat 500 or 600 calories for two days a week and don't significantly overcompensate during the remaining five days (as evidence shows most people don't), it stands to reason that weight will start to fall off. But research suggests that intermittent fasting may help people remove excess weight in a more efficient and effective way than normal calorie restriction.

In particular, a 2011 review by researchers at the University of Illinois at Chicago found that people who did alternate day fasting (a repeating pattern of one day unrestricted eating followed by one day of no- or low-calorie fasting) were more likely to retain higher amounts of muscle tissue while losing at least as much fat. This is important because muscle helps to keep your metabolic rate higher, in essence because it is much more metabolically active than other tissues. In short, by having a more muscular frame you can continue to burn more calories all day every day, even when you are sitting down or sleeping, which is very helpful in managing your weight over the longer term.

What doesn't kill you makes you stronger

Research published in the *Journal of Nutritional Biochemistry* showed that feeding rats and mice only every other day improved the health and function of their brains, hearts and other organs. Other studies have shown that mice and rats on intermittent fasts develop fewer cancers, are less prone to neurological disorders and live 30 per cent longer than their siblings that were fed every day. All this is fascinating stuff that's driving the new wave of human studies, but what's particularly interesting is that experts think it's the *stress* that fasting puts on the body that does the good!

According to Professor Mark Mattson – reported by *New Scientist* magazine to be the world's most cited neuroscientist – fasting is a type of hormesis, a process whereby organisms exposed to low levels of stress or toxins become more resistant to tougher challenges. For example, the mild biological stress induced by fasting causes cells in the heart and gut to produce proteins that decrease heart rate and blood pressure and increase gut motility (the movement of food through the gut), reducing the risk of heart disease, stroke and colon cancer. It really does seem to be a case of what doesn't kill you (i.e., managing on minimum food for a couple of days a week) makes you stronger!

Diabetes and blood sugar control

Any amount of weight loss in obese individuals, however it is achieved, will generally result in the body becoming more sensitive to insulin, which is an important step towards reducing the risk of diabetes (exercise has the effect of making you more responsive to insulin, too). But intermittent fasting could have a particularly good effect on your blood sugar control and diabetes risk.

In one of Dr Michelle Harvie's studies for Genesis Breast Cancer Prevention at Manchester's Wyntheshawe Hospital, women who were on a 5:2-style intermittent fasting diet (largely milk and vegetables, adding up to 650 calories for two days each week, and a Mediterranean-style diet for the rest of the time), were compared with women who were restricted to 1,500 calories every day. In both groups women lost weight, reduced their cholesterol levels, recorded lower blood pressures and had reduced markers of breast cancer risk. When it came to reductions in fasting insulin and insulin resistance – both signs that diabetes risk has decreased – the benefits, though modest, were greater in the 5:2 diet group than those using conventional calorie restriction.

Heart disease

As I have alluded to, a reduction in cardiovascular risk factors – for example, LDL cholesterol (that's the 'bad' type that carries cholesterol towards arteries, where it collects and causes 'furring') and high blood pressure – can be expected on the 5:2 diet. Triglycerides in the blood will also tend to fall as you lose weight (put simply, this means that your blood is less sticky and therefore less liable to clot).

Much of the work in this area has been done by Dr Krista Varady and her team at the University of Illinois at Chicago, with one of her scientific papers on the subject being entitled 'Intermittent fasting combined with calorie restriction is effective for weight loss and cardio-protection in obese women' (November 2012). The research outlines how intermittent fasting, and wider, healthy weight loss, can benefit heart health. It's all very much in the title really!

Brain function

Much of the research into intermittent fasting actually started, and continues, in the healthy ageing field, and brain ageing in particular. At the National Institute on Aging in America they've been investigating rats and mice that have been genetically engineered to develop Alzheimer's disease. Given normal circumstances, these animals show obvious signs of dementia by the time they are a year old (getting disorientated in a maze that they have previously been able to navigate with ease, for example), but when they're put on an on/off fasting regimen they don't develop dementia until they're around 20 months, or much nearer the natural end of their lives.

What could be the reason? One thing that's been reported is that the fasting mouse brain produces more of a protein called BDNF (brain-derived neurotrophic factor), which stimulates the growth of new nerve cells in the hippocampus part of the brain, essential for learning and memory. There's certainly an evolutionary logic for the fasting state to be linked with better cognitive function, too: if you were hungry in caveman days, you needed your wits about you to track down the next meal and survive!

As yet there are still many unknowns (for example, whether longer periods of fasting are needed than normally experienced on a 5:2 diet) and the human studies have still to be done, so it's impossible to say if intermittent fasting will help to prevent dementia. But it's certainly a very interesting area of research, and one to watch.

Cancer

Much of the published research into the potential disease-protective effects of intermittent fasting involve measuring a biological marker named insulin-like growth factor-1 (IGF-1), which is known to be associated with cancer. Fasting has the effect of reducing IGF-1 levels, at least temporarily, and also seems to stimulate genes that repair our cells.

How a reduction in IGF-1 translates into successful real-world outcomes (i.e., a reduced chance of people getting cancer) is still unclear, however. One 2007 clinical review did look at 'real-world' health outcomes and concluded that intermittent fasting (specifically, alternate day fasting, which usually has minimum 18-hour periods without food) may have a protective effect against cancer, as well as heart disease and diabetes. However, it concluded 'research is required to establish definitively the consequences', which is a fair reflection of the science as it currently is. In short, how effective intermittent fasting is against cancer relative to other healthy-eating or weight-loss regimens is still to be clarified.

COULD 5:2 MAKE YOU HAPPIER?

Anecdotally, many 5:2 eaters say their low-calorie intake makes them feel more clear-headed, more able to concentrate and even more cheerful. It's uncertain as to why this should be, but feeling more upbeat will certainly make it easier to refuse that slice of cake!

Getting started

The beauty of the 5:2 diet is that, beyond the requirement for two 500- or 600-calorie days a week, there are no firm rules and it's very flexible. As with all new healthy habits, however, it can take time to adjust and the hunger aspect can initially be hard. On the plus side, the results you begin to see and feel within short order mean your fast days will quickly become less of a chore, and even something you can begin to enjoy. Preparation and planning are key.

Choose your fasting days

As a first step, you'll need to decide which days will work best for you as fasting days. This may evolve over time, or from week to week, according to your circumstances. As a general rule, you're more likely to stick to the regimen if you can repeat the same two days every week, so try to choose days that you'll need to deviate from only infrequently. For example, don't pick a Tuesday if this is the day when a friend is most likely to invite you round for lunch, or a Friday if you're going to be tempted by a takeaway after work. For obvious reasons, weekend days may not be such good fasting days either, but everyone's different and you should choose what works for you.

Whether you run the two days consecutively or apart is also up to you, and there isn't enough research to say definitively that one way or another is best. Many people doing 5:2 for themselves, rather than in the context of a highly monitored clinical trial, find it easiest in terms of managing hunger and keeping on track to have a gap between fasting days. Having this breather between days helps you feel your dieting task is neither too hard nor too long. However, it may be that you're more likely to get the two days done if you run them back to back. If doing two days together suits you better, and you feel energetic and motivated, there's no reason why you shouldn't do it this way (and it may even be better for your body).

THE GENDER DIVIDE

On a fasting day:

- If you're a man, you should have no more than 600 calories.
- If you're a woman, you should have no more than 500 calories.
- It is a fact that, even if a man and a woman weigh the same, the man will usually burn more calories than the woman because he has a higher proportion of muscle (see page 8).

Fast day meals

The second decision to make is how you will spread your 500 or 600 calories over the fasting day. Again, this is down to personal preference, usually honed through trial and error. A satisfying format for many people is to bookend their day with two meals – a 100–200-calorie breakfast and a 300-calorie dinner for example, with the possibility of 100 calories or so for snacking or another small meal in between if desired. Other people report they are happier if they don't eat their first morsel until brunch or lunch, while still others (usually men, on anecdotal evidence) prefer saving up their calories for just one reasonable-sized meal – either a lunch or an evening meal.

One argument for leaving your first calorie intake until lunch or later is that the stretch of time you go without food is longer – perhaps 18 hours or more – which some researchers have surmised may be associated with potentially bigger health benefits (see page 9). (By comparison, the longest you'd go without food if you eat breakfast on your fasting day is likely to be around 12 hours.)

However, many people, perhaps women in particular, prefer to graze their way through fast days, and Dr Michelle Harvie's research offers some reassurance here. It found that obese women eating three small, evenly spaced mini meals on two non-consecutive fasting days per week lost weight efficiently and also reduced inflammatory chemicals that increase breast cancer risk.

The main point is to find what suits you and not to shoehorn yourself into a routine that doesn't fit your lifestyle. We simply don't know the optimum food-free stretch, if there is any optimum at all.

Keep a food diary

To find a pattern of food intake that enables you to stick to your 5:2 plans and achieve sustainable weight loss, try keeping a food and mood diary. Making a note of how you feel physically and mentally on fast days can be an effective way to track how well you're coping with the regimen. Simply jot down what foods/meals you eat, when you have them and any accompanying feelings of hunger, mood or wavering will power. Registering when you feel at your weakest and strongest on a fast day can help you to tailor future fast days so that they are easier.

What does 500 calories look like?

Admittedly not a lot – but then that is, after all, somewhat the point! As a rough guide, 500 calories would be:

- Breakfast: A small bowl (30 g/1 oz) of bran flakes with 125 ml (4 fl oz) semi-skimmed milk, plus a handful (80 g/3 oz) each of blueberries and strawberries (200 calories).
- Dinner: Half a 400 g (13 oz) can of bean soup followed by 100 g (3½ oz) prawns with a dessert bowl of salad of rocket, peppers, tomato and cucumber dressed with 1 tablespoon of low-fat balsamic dressing (250 calories).
- Snack: ½ banana (50 calories).
- Men have another 100 calories to play with, which is the equivalent of adding half a slice of toast spread with 1 scant dessertspoon of peanut butter.

If this looks daunting, don't worry – there are lots of tips for making your fasting day as painless as possible in the following pages. While most intermittent fasters will find it challenging at first, the process gets much easier as your body adapts.

More than 500 or 600 calories?

Some regimes allow up to 700 calories on fast days, but if you increase calories on these two days you'll probably have to look at introducing some restrictions on the other five days, too. The amount of 500 or 600 calories is 25 per cent of the normal average calorie requirement, and emulates the protocol used by some preliminary but successful alternate day fasting human studies completed at the University of Illinois at Chicago (a 5:2 fasting regimen is a more achievable version of alternate day fasting, and you'll probably find it easier to stick to).

While a handful of calories either way isn't going to make much difference, if it becomes obvious you're going to breach 500 or 600 calories by a large amount, abandon ship and count the day as a non-fast one.

TOP TIPS FOR BEGINNERS

- The day before your first fast, eat well and aim to go to bed feeling neither hungry nor overfull. Getting an early night is good preparation. Trying to stuff in as much food as late as possible so you don't feel hungry tomorrow is not!
- Do your eating homework so that you know how you are going to spend your 500 or 600 calories, and which meals you are going to spread them between. Use the recipes in this book as inspiration and make sure you are stocked up with the requisite ingredients.
- Try to make your environment as devoid of food temptations as possible, which means ensuring a stray slice of pork pie isn't the thing screaming, 'eat me!' when you open the fridge.
- Arm yourself with some kind of calorie counter – there is one to get you started on pages 140–142 – or you can use an online app or website.
- Be aware that choosing a less busy day to start your fasting may not be the best approach. As long as you have your food choices pre-planned, a day with plenty to keep you occupied may be better.
- If you find your first fast too hard and have to give in, you've probably just chosen the wrong day. Don't despair and try again another time, but leave it a few days.

Fast day eating

Theoretically you could have a large burger and endless cups of black coffee on a fast day and be within your calorie allowance, but clearly this wouldn't be at all good for you! Instead, it's a great idea to use your fasting day to make balanced and healthy choices, using the following guidelines.

Eat five a day

Your fast day is the perfect opportunity to fill up on fruit and veg as these foods are bulky and low in calories, take up plenty of room on your plate (a psychological boost!) and are linked with a lower risk of killer diseases such as heart disease and cancer. Green leafy vegetables, such as spinach, kale, watercress, rocket, broccoli and cabbage, are particularly low in calories, as are berries, such as strawberries, raspberries, blackcurrants and redcurrants, which you'll often find in convenient form in the freezer section of the supermarket. Tomatoes, peppers, orange-fleshed melons and butternut squash join the low-calorie corner – the wonderful thing about all these richly coloured fruit and veg is they consistently appear in superfood lists because of their high antioxidant content (antioxidants are the component in fruit and veg that mop up the free radicals that can damage our cells).

In short, by using your fast day as a chance to eat at least five colourful portions of fruit and veg a day (a portion is around 80 g/3 oz, or roughly a handful), you'll be boosting your health as well as benefiting your waistline.

Dairy and pulses

These two deserve a special mention because they're unusual in providing a combination of carbs and protein in one easy package and are a great source of vitamins and minerals. They can be easy on the waistline too – 0% Greek yogurt (a great topping for fruit) has only 57 calories in a 100 g (3½ oz) serving, while creamy canned butter beans (fabulous to bulk out a salad) have 56 calories in a 60 g (2½ oz) serving.

Include lean protein

The lowest calorie lean protein sources (all weighing in at less than 100 calories for a 100 g/3½ oz portion) include prawns, tofu and tuna canned in water, though grilled fish, eggs and chicken breast are also very good choices. Including one or more of these protein foods on a fast day is to be recommended, as you're more likely to preserve valuable muscle tissue during periods of calorie restriction when protein is consumed (exercising helps conserve muscle tissue too). Another big bonus is that protein is particularly good at keeping you full, so can help to keep hunger pangs at bay for longer. Digesting it also uses up more calories than does digesting other nutrients, which is all grist to the mill of your diminishing middle!

Choose quality carbs

Admittedly you won't be able to eat very big carb portions on a fast day (there are around 100 calories in just one slice of bread, for example), but it's a good idea to make sure any modest portions you do choose are as unprocessed or nutrient rich as possible, and to focus on higher fibre choices where you can. Wholemeal breads, porridge oats, wholewheat pasta, pearl barley, fortified wholegrain breakfast cereals and potatoes in their skins tend to have a relatively low glycaemic index or GI, which means they raise blood sugar levels only relatively slowly, helping to keep blood sugar, energy and appetite levels more controlled.

Though sticking to the correct quantity of calories is the key priority on fast day, the quality of those calories is important too, so try not to get sidetracked by too many sweet foods. We've included a few sweet treats you can get away with and enjoy in the recipe section, but too many high GI, very sugary carbs can really challenge your ability to stay on track because they can cause your blood sugar levels to fluctuate, heightening feelings of hunger.

Drink options

It is important to stay well hydrated on fast days (see page 28), but with the exception of low-fat milk (or a milk alternative, such as soya milk), many drinks can be a wasteful, non-filling way to spend calories. Your best options on a fast day are calorie-free drinks, such

---

PERFECT FAST DAY PROPORTIONS

- Concentrate on fruit and veg (steamed, grilled, stir-fried or in soups and salads) as your main stomach-filling priority (up to 200 calories).
- Most of the remaining calories (300 or 400) will be best spent on low GI carbohydrate-rich and/or protein-rich foods.
- Any calories you have left over you can use as you wish (see the lists of up to 50 calorie and up to 100 calorie snack suggestions on pages 36–37). But choosing more nutritious foods is always best.

as black coffee and tea (though try not to drink more caffeine than you would normally), herbal teas, diet drinks and of course (and best of all), good old water. To jazz it up, try a sparkling variety and add a squeeze of lime or lemon.

Alcohol is one of the least sensible choices of all (even the smallest glass of wine has around 100 calories and could stimulate your appetite) so use your fast days to abstain from alcohol altogether and give your liver two days a week of much needed rest!

Fast day feel-full tips

- Water is the perfect slimline filler, either drunk on its own to temporarily take the edge off a hunger pang or, more particularly, incorporated within food to increase satiety (the feeling of fullness that food imparts). Chunky soups plus lots of fruit and veg can work particularly well on a fast day because they'll help to make your stomach feel full.
- Airy foods take up more space on your plate (so, psychologically, it feels like you're being presented with more food), as well as in your stomach. One study by Professor Barbara Rolls at Pennsylvania State University, published in the journal *Appetite*, compared the same snack in a puffed and non-puffed version and found that those receiving the airy snack ate 73 per cent more in volume, but consumed 21 per cent fewer calories. Rice cakes are the ultimate airy food, and a whipped mousse (which can have fewer than 80 calories per pot) is ok for a quick dessert if you can't do without!
- Protein-rich foods are particularly good at inducing satiety. One theory is that they stimulate the release of hunger-controlling hormones in the gut. The protein in eggs seems particularly good at keeping you full, so give them a try!
- Wholegrain versions of breakfast cereals, breads, pasta, rice and noodles take longer to chew and are more satisfying, as the fibre they contain provides bulk but no calories. Fibre also has a slowing effect on the passage of food through the gut, which has the effect of keeping you fuller for longer. The portion size of bread or pasta you can have on a fast day is small, but choosing a 'brown', not 'white', version can help to make it more filling.
- Focus on foods made from scratch. On average, foods that aren't highly processed, pre-packaged or high in sugar will tend to be lower GI and keep your blood sugar levels on a more even keel.

Don't estimate!

Building up an accurate picture of what actually constitutes 500 or 600 calories (see page 16) is one of the most educational and interesting aspects of the 5:2 diet. It can help you understand what constitutes a healthy portion and might also give a clue as to why you ended up needing to lose a few pounds in the first place.

It won't come as a surprise, then, that 'estimates' and 'educated guesses' are definitely not okay when it comes to calculating your fast day calories. With the best will in the world you'll almost certainly be wrong, which will jeopardize your weight loss and dilute the

WHAT ABOUT SWEETENERS?

Sugar substitutes, including aspartame, sucralose and more recently stevia, have been approved by the UK government and health authorities the world over, yet there still seems to be a host of scare stories circulating as to how they could actually make us fatter or even cause cancer. In the end it's up to you if you want to use them or not, but if adding a bit of sweetness to a bowl of berries or to a cup of tea makes you more inclined to stay on track with your 5:2 diet, then go ahead and use them. Unless you're eating sweeteners in vast quantities they are very unlikely to do any harm and are a much better bet on fast day than spoonfuls of sugar.

health benefits. If you're not convinced, try seeing if you can correctly estimate the 'recommended' 30 g (1 oz) serving of flake-style breakfast cereal, such as bran flakes. Most people pour nearer to 50–60 g (2–2½ oz) into the bowl, which can add over 100 'accidental' calories and completely destroy a fasting day. If you don't own weighing scales and a measuring jug, you need to lay your hands on both. With a basic set of electronic kitchen scales available at relatively low cost, and measuring jugs even cheaper, it doesn't require a great investment. Make sure you also have some measuring spoons in your kitchen drawer and you'll be well fixed.

At first, you should weigh everything until you've got a clearer idea of what different-sized portions weigh. Your idea of a 'medium-sized' apple – 100 g (3½ oz) with peel but no core, according to official publications – may be very different to mine or someone else's. It's also important to weigh the ingredients carefully when you're making the recipes in this book, so they don't exceed the calorie counts given. If it seems like a pain, it's really not – it's actually quite fun learning about calories and portion sizes and, as you're only doing it two days a week and you're not eating terribly much on those days either, it's not at all onerous. Look at it as a chance to really understand what you are putting into your mouth.

'OFF' DAY EATING

Of necessity, some time has been spent explaining about fasting days, what to eat on them and how to make sure they're successful. But let's not forget that the beauty of 5:2, and the core reason that it appeals to, and works for, so many people, is that you can have five days each week without worrying about cutting a single calorie!

Does that mean you can truly eat anything you want too? Well, yes, but naturally there are limits. The good news? Studies consistently show that contrary to what you might expect, intermittent fasters are actually very unlikely to go on a big binge on their 'off' days. Rather than make your appetite more extreme, 5:2 dieting seems to help naturally regulate it so you enjoy only as much food as you need when you aren't fasting. That said, if your journey to 5:2 eating has involved a lifetime of flip-flopping between failed diets and bingeing, it may take longer for a healthy relationship with food to develop.

What to expect on the 5:2 diet

If you have a BMI of 25 or more (use an online calculator to check your BMI) when you start your 5:2 eating plan you can expect to lose weight at an average rate of 500 g (1 lb) a week until you stabilize at a healthy weight within the 18.5–25 BMI range. However, as with any form of calorie restriction, the amount you lose will vary from week to week, so expect highs, lows and plateaus along the way. In the beginning you may lose weight quite quickly – 1–1.5 kg (2–3 lb) isn't unusual in the first week – which can be hugely motivating. The flipside is that you risk becoming despondent in the weeks that follow if your weight loss fluctuates or slows down.

The key to success is always to have the bigger picture in mind – there may be disappointments along the way, but all the evidence suggests that in the longer term you will succeed. While the path may not be entirety smooth, no other slim-down regimen can boast that you can eat without calorie restriction for five days a week and still be 6.35 kg (14 lb) lighter in three to four months.

Measuring your progress

Before you begin the 5:2 diet, it's a good idea to know what your starting point is so you can measure your progress along the way. Some people say they prefer not to use scales and are happy just to measure their progress in terms of a looser waistband, but this can often be about denial. No one is forcing you to weigh and measure, but if your weight has been creeping ever upwards and you haven't been tracking it, it is probably best to bite the bullet, get on those scales and face up to what your starting point may be.

MONITORING YOUR WEIGHT
Research findings from America's National Weight Control Registry – a database of people who have maintained a weight loss of 13.6 kg (30 lb) or more for at least one year or more – show that 75 per cent of weight-watchers use regular weighing as part of their success strategy, and most diet and health professionals now believe that weekly monitoring of weight is a marker of diet success.

Many bathrooms scales will also give you a read-out of your percentage body fat, which should show a pleasing downward trend as the weeks go by. Do be aware that different scales can give quite different body fat readings, however, and even the same scales will register ups and downs from one day to the next, depending on factors such as time of day and how much fluid you've consumed. As with your weight, it's the trend over time that matters, so don't get hung up over individual measurements. Even small reductions in internal fat lower heart disease and diabetes risk.

WAIST MEASUREMENT

Another simple but effective way to measure your progress is with a tape measure around your middle. Measure at the place where your waist is naturally narrowest or, if this is hard to define, at the midpoint between the top of your hip bone and the bottom of your ribs. This measurement is a reasonable proxy for the amount of internal fat you have in the central region and in turn a good marker for heart disease, high blood pressure and diabetes risk. As your waist measurement falls, your risk of developing any of these conditions is steadily reduced.

For men, risk moves from high to medium as waist measurement falls below 102 cm (40 inches) and to low risk when the measurement goes below 94 cm (37 inches). For women, the respective figures are 88 cm (34½ inches) and 80 cm (31½ inches). People of Asian backgrounds tend to have a higher proportion of body fat to muscle and need to achieve smaller waist measurements than those of Caucasians to achieve the same level of risk reduction.

AVAILABLE TESTS

As you progress with 5:2 fasting and the weight continues to drop off, you can also expect your level of LDL cholesterol (see page 12) to decrease, your blood pressure to come down and your blood glucose level to shift downwards. Other biomarkers – for example, those that predict cancer risk (see page 13) – will also be likely to improve.

Overstretched medical practitioners tend not to be best pleased when 'worried well' patients demand repeated tests for no good medical reason. And less run-of-the-mill blood tests – for example, for IGF-1, which has been tracked in some intermittent fasting trials – aren't available in the UK on the NHS. However, your health care practitioner may be happy to do simple but important checks on your blood pressure and cholesterol level, both now and after you've lost about 6.5 kg (14 lb) or so. If not, some pharmacies offer a fully validated cholesterol check, which is relatively inexpensive.

Dealing with hunger

At first, those gripey hunger pangs can seem quite insistent on fast days. But the good news is that those feelings definitely become much less intense, with most long-term 5:2 devotees stating that they are no longer unduly troubled by fast day hunger after a few weeks. Another possibility is that intermittent fasters simply learn to embrace the feeling and not to be fazed by it.

Getting on top of initial hunger pangs can be as simple as actually experiencing those feelings and realizing that you can come out the other side without collapsing in a heap on the floor or dying of starvation! We're so programmed to eat at the slightest twinge of hunger that feeling anything more than slightly peckish can actually be quite alien and even a little bit scary. In time, when you realize nothing dreadful is going to happen if you feel hungry for a day, this will change and you can actually learn to appreciate the physical sensations of hunger you get on a fast day, knowing that you are in tune with your body and have tackled the art of being able to savour food without overloading your system.

Exercise and 5:2

An exercise programme can definitely complement your 5:2 weight-loss progress, and will provide many attendant health benefits, such as stronger bones and a healthier heart. But how should you negotiate exercise on a fast day? The old wisdom was that you should be well fuelled prior to exercise but the latest evidence suggests that modest activity in the fasted state is actually good for you. In particular, exercising in the fasted state means that the body has to use fat as its primary fuel, which is good news for the disappearance of those love handles! Another benefit of exercising on an empty

stomach appears to be that you'll build muscle better when you do get round to eating in the post-exercise period.

In a nutshell, there's no reason you shouldn't work out on your fast day, with the ideal being to exercise when you are feeling hungry, perhaps in the afternoon, and then to follow with one of your fast day meals. However, common sense must come into play and if you're new to exercise it's probably best to ease yourself into physical activity on non-fast days only. There's also some suggestion that women are better doing weights on fasting days (while men can particularly benefit from cardio work). Listening to your body is essential, and you should always stop exercising immediately if you feel faint, dizzy or light-headed.

HOW ACTIVE SHOULD I BE?

Official guidelines suggest that for optimum health benefits you should be physically active (at the level of brisk walking or gentle cycling, for example) for at least 30 minutes five times a week. If you're doing something more vigorous, such as running or playing a racquet sport, you can get away with 75 minutes, or three 25-minute sessions a week. On top of this, one or two 20-minute sessions with weights are also recommended to maintain muscle tone and lean tissue levels, particularly in the over 40s.

10 ways to make the 5:2 diet work for you

1 Be flexible

The 5:2 regimen is definitely not a prescriptive diet with a big list of 'dos' and 'don'ts' that you may have been used to in the past. That's a plus point, but it can also be a tad off-putting at first if you're used to being told exactly what you can and can't do as part of a weight-loss regimen.

The secret to finding the version for you is to be prepared to road test different fasting day routines until you find the one that works best. When it comes down to it, the chance to change fasting days around is the key attraction of 5:2 and you should feel free to exploit that flexibility to it's fullest. One of the key deciding factors as to whether a diet works for you is how easily it fits around your existing lifestyle. This one of the key reasons why 5:2 attracts and retains followers.

2 Keep well hydrated

Fluid is your friend on fast days as it helps to give a sensation of stomach fullness, at least temporarily. As it's also possible to confuse hunger with thirst, keeping up your intake of fluids at all times will prevent you falling foul of this potentially waist-widening mix-up. As a bonus, water is needed for every chemical reaction in the body, including burning fat.

Don't think you must stick to plain water if you don't want to, though – black tea and coffee, herbal tea and calorie-free beverages all count towards your fluid intake, too.

Most fresh fruit is over 85 per cent water and contains fibre so is good at keeping you both hydrated and full.

3 Find a fasting buddy

Research shows that when you're tackling your weight you'll do better if you have someone doing it alongside you. For example, a study at the University of Pennsylvania found that 66 per cent of the people dieting with friends had maintained their weight loss after 10 months compared to only 24 per cent of those who were dieting on their own.

There's no particular reason that you'll need more support with 5:2 than any other regimen, and in fact many people do it quite successfully all by themselves as the periods of food deprivation are short and manageable. However, if a partner or friend wants to do it with you, you should jump at the chance for the extra support it brings.

4 Keep out of temptation's way

Fasting days are surprisingly doable, and with a positive mindset and some forward menu planning you can even sit down for an evening meal (albeit with a different mix of foods on your plate) with the rest of the family. But – and it's a big and fairly logical but – there's simply no point putting yourself in temptation's way if you can avoid it!

Research at Cornell University's Food and Brand Lab in America has identified visibility and convenience as the two biggest drivers of mindless eating, with 'out of sight' being a key strategy to successful calorie control. So taking steps as simple as keeping biscuits in an opaque container or in a drawer, or moving a bowl of sweets from your office desk to a filing cabinet a distance away can markedly increase your chances of staying on track on a fast day.

However, if you are faced with a food temptation, psychologists believe tightening muscles is so closely tied to determination that simply doing it can muster up greater will power to resist. In studies, subjects were more likely to think they could resist chocolate cake while flexing their biceps, while others were better able to resist unhealthy foods at a snack bar while holding a pen woven through spread fingers (thus engaging their hand muscles). It's not hard to imagine how clenching helps, and balling your fists is certainly worth a try when faced with a strong temptation to break your fast!

5 Save chocolate for 'off' days

Quite apart from the fact that you'll only be able to have a disappointingly teeny amount, one small study has suggested that eating chocolate when we are hungry may heighten our general desire for it. Conversely, eating it when we are full may 'train' us out of a craving. Researchers at University College London split students into two groups, giving both groups half a bar of chocolate twice a day. After two weeks, the half that had been told to eat their chocolate rations on an empty stomach reported a stronger craving than before. By contrast, the students who had been eating the chocolate on a full stomach craved chocolate less and even reported that it now seemed somewhat less pleasant to the taste.

6 Consider an internet food shop

Patrolling the aisles with your trolley can give you a small amount of exercise, but you may find that it's better to do an internet shop and go for a run instead! The reason? When you're shopping for fast day food, supermarkets can be a toxic environment in the sense that the sights, smells and deli counters can lure you to put things in your basket that you hadn't got on your list and didn't intend to buy. On your five 'off' days, you can of course choose whatever foods you want, but many people do find they start to develop a natural inclination to eat a more balanced and healthy diet overall, which internet shopping is potentially more supportive of. Certainly, if your grocery shop starts to involve lots of label reading (often in a challenging font size!), it may be easier to do this food-sleuthing at the click of a mouse rather than in the supermarket itself.

7 Stay positive about weight loss

Virtually all people trying to lose weight will experience phases when they continue to stay at the same weight for what seems like a frustratingly long period of time. In actuality it's likely to be only a few weeks, and anecdotally 5:2 eaters seem to experience fewer plateaus, possibly because of the constant switch between higher and lower calorie intakes and because levels of lean tissue (with a higher energy expenditure than fat) are maintained. However, if you do experience a plateau, a positive mindset is key. Try to focus on the weight you have lost and consider every week that you stick with your fast days as a success that's worth patting yourself on the back for. Traditional 'diets' often aren't sustainable, but with 5:2 you should find it easier to keep on keeping on, such that you do succeed in the end! In reality, it's only plateaus that happen early on that tend to be a problem. Most established 5:2 fans are so wedded to their routine, weight loss becomes purely a bonus. On a practical level, shifting your activity level up a gear can help shake you out of a plateau. It's good to vary your routine too, as your body will work harder at something it is not accustomed to.

8 Get more sleep

The evidence that insufficient sleep correlates to higher body weight has been piling up, and the latest strand of evidence suggests junk food may be particularly appealing to tired brains. When scientists at St Luke's-Roosevelt Hospital Center and Columbia University in New York used high-tech brain scans to measure responses to unhealthy foods (like pepperoni pizza and sweets) versus healthier options (porridge and fruit), they found that the brain's reward centre lit up more at the sight of junk food if the subjects tested were fatigued.

The take-home message? Get plenty of sleep, particularly the night before a fast day. At the very least it's good for your general wellbeing; at best it may also help keep up your resolve to stick with 5:2.

9 Keep busy

The devil may make work for idle hands, but you're also more likely to end up with your hands in the biscuit tin if you're bored or not very busy. Part of planning a successful fasting day is therefore thinking what you will do to occupy yourself as well as what you will eat. The most successful days are those when you have a particularly engrossing work project, are focusing on caring for children or (hopefully this will happen from time to time), just enjoying a day out.

10 Don't be hard on yourself

If you have to miss a few fasting days because of holidays or other life events, don't beat yourself up. There's always tomorrow or next week and you're meant to be living a life, not enduring a life sentence!

5:2 for life

Once you've reached the weight you're happy with, what next? As you've read through these pages, I hope you've become convinced that intermittent fasting, or 5:2, could well be something you incorporate into your life long term, as an active lifestyle choice. When bigger, longer studies into intermittent fasting emerge, as they undoubtedly will, the optimal way to continue intermittent fasting so that you can maximize any health benefits and keep your weight maintained will almost certainly become more apparent.

For now, the consensus approach from most people doing 5:2 who have already reached their ideal weight and don't wish to become any slimmer is to switch to 500- or 600-calorie fasting just one day a week (a 6:1 diet!). A small study showed people who had lost weight could keep it off by doing this, though another approach, if you want to keep a slightly firmer watch on your weight, would be to continue with two fast days – but let them creep up to 700 calories, say.

Some people may find they can manage by using 5:2 fasting now and again (intermittent intermittent fasting, if you like!), or to stop for longer periods or even altogether. These folk will be the ones who have become confident that they can now trust their own eating intuition to keep them safe from weight gain. In short, they can now trust their inbuilt hunger and fullness mechanisms (that were there all the time!) to stay happily at their optimum weight.

Whatever your approach, remember that you should always obtain pleasure from your eating and your diet should never become a terrible chore. If you choose intermittent fasting as your ongoing method of optimizing health and weight, the recipes and suggested plans that follow should make that eminently possible, for as long as you choose.

4-week fast day meal planner

Week 1		
Day 1		
Breakfast	1 poached egg on half a slice of wholemeal toast spread with 1 teaspoon of low-fat spread and 1 medium (85 g/3 oz) tomato, grilled	163 calories
Lunch or snack	1 rounded tablespoon (30 g/1 oz) of tzatziki with 100 g (3½ oz) cucumber and red pepper sticks	60 calories
Dinner	Asian Steamed Chicken Salad (see page 94)	273 calories
		496 calories

If you're a man: Add a very small handful (19 g/½ oz) of plain peanuts to the chicken salad

Day 2		
Breakfast	1 Blueberry Bran Muffin (see page 45)	142 calories
Lunch or snack	1 apple and 1 satsuma	75 calories
Dinner	Red Mullet with Baked Tomatoes (see page 99)	287 calories
		504 calories

If you're a man: Add a bowl (300 g/10 oz) of shop-bought fresh carrot and coriander soup at lunch

Week 2		
Day 1		
Breakfast	30 g (1 oz) serving of bran flakes with 125 ml (4 fl oz) semi-skimmed milk and a handful (80 g/3 oz) of blueberries	180 calories
Lunch or snack	2 clementines and 1 kiwifruit	73 calories
Dinner	Butternut Squash & Ricotta Frittata (see page 68)	248 calories
		501 calories

If you're a man: Serve yourself a bigger bowl of cereal (55 g/2 oz bran flakes and 175 ml/6 fl oz semi-skimmed milk) at breakfast

Day 2

Breakfast	½ plain bagel topped with 30 g (1 oz) light soft cheese and 50 g (2 oz) smoked salmon	270 calories
Lunch or snack	1 slice of cantaloupe melon and 1 clementine	45 calories
Dinner	Aromatic Steamed Mussels (see page 108)	185 calories
		500 calories

If you're a man: Top the melon with 2–3 slices of Parma ham

Week 3

Day 1

Breakfast	Porridge made with 50 g (2 oz) oats and 200 ml (7 fl oz) skimmed milk, plus 80 g (3 oz) raspberries. Add sweetener, if liked	269 calories
Lunch or snack	1 large plum, about 90 g/3½ oz (weighed with stone)	31 calories
Dinner	Fish & Tomato Curry (see page 105) with a handful of watercress leaves	199 calories
		499 calories

If you're a man: Add half a slice of toast spread with 1 scant dessertspoon (10 g/⅓ oz) of peanut butter

Day 2

Breakfast	1 medium apple	53 calories
Lunch or snack	Lime & Ginger Prawn Coleslaw (see page 74)	143 calories
Dinner	Masala Roast Cod (see page 98) followed by a rhubarb bake	300 calories
		496 calories

If you're a man: Have 2 plain poppadums with the cod

Week 4

Day 1

Breakfast	1 slice of wholemeal toast spread with 1 teaspoon of low-fat spread and yeast extract, and a bowl of raspberries (90 g/3½ oz)	147 calories
Lunch or snack	95 g (3½ oz) can skinless, boneless sardines in tomato sauce on a bed of bagged green leaves, and 100 g (3½ oz) cherry tomatoes	183 calories
Dinner	Russian Meatballs (see page 113) with 7 cherry tomatoes	169 calories
		499 calories

If you're a man: Have the sardines on a slice of toast

Day 2

Breakfast	Fruity Summer Milkshake (see page 40)	89 calories
Lunch or snack	1 rounded tablespoon (30 g/1 oz) of tzatziki with 100 g (3½ oz) cucumber and red pepper sticks	60 calories
Dinner	Lemony Scallop Skewers (see page 107) followed by Strawberry Roulade (see page 138)	348 calories
		497 calories

If you're a man: Add a banana

PORTION PERFECTION

Tasty meals are your absolute ally on fast day, but if something tastes too nice you need to watch yourself carefully! Making sure you are scrupulous with portion sizes when you're serving up the recipes is important. Choosing dishes that just serve one may be a best if you're dieting solo and can't be sure you have enough self control.

Give yourself a treat

50 snacks up to 100 calories

- 1 medium apple (125 g/4 oz weighed whole): 53 calories
- 15 g (½ oz) plain almonds (around 9 nuts, but weigh them as they vary): 88 calories
- 1 warm crumpet spread with yeast extract (no butter): 100 calories
- 15 g (½ oz) salted popcorn: 83 calories
- 100 g (3½ oz) shop-bought lemon and coriander prawns: 80 calories
- 1 slice of Parma ham wrapped around a breadstick: 58 calories
- 1 rye crispbread with 30 g (1 oz) light soft cheese: 82 calories
- 1 individually wrapped mini malt loaf (for lunch boxes): 95 calories
- 50 g (2 oz) (¼ pot) reduced-fat prawn cocktail: 83 calories
- 15 g (½ oz) roasted, salted peanuts: 89 calories
- 1 rounded tablespoon (30 g/1 oz) of tzatziki with 100 g (3½ oz) cucumber and red pepper sticks: 60 calories
- 100 g (3½ oz) fat-free strawberry yogurt: 79 calories
- 1 light cheese triangle and 1 slice of cucumber spread on 1 oatcake: 82 calories
- 1 medium banana: 95 calories
- 200 g (7 oz) canned lentil soup: 95 calories
- 1 falafel with 1 teaspoon of sweet chilli sauce: 65 calories
- 70 g (3 oz) cooked chicken tikka breast pieces: 90 calories
- 1 cold Quorn Cumberland sausage: 86 calories
- 1 Quorn goujon with 2 teaspoons of sweet chilli dipping sauce: 87 calories
- 12 g (½ oz) Brazil nuts: 82 calories (2 nuts, but weigh them as they vary)
- 20 g (¾ oz) wafer-thin ham, 1 tomato and a little mustard: 81 calories

- 1 small glass (150 ml/¼ pint) low-fat strawberry milkshake: 90 calories
- ½ pomegranate: 55 calories
- 1 sesame rice cake with 7 g (¼ oz) tahini: 74 calories
- 75 g (3 oz) ready-cooked tikka-flavoured chicken breast fillets: 98 calories
- 1 slice of fruit loaf: 98 calories
- 50 g (2 oz) mashed avocado flesh sprinkled with lime juice: 100 calories
- 50 g (2 oz) reduced-fat hummus with cucumber sticks: 100 calories
- 1 pack of cheesy-flavoured corn puffs: 96 calories
- 1 pack of baked cheese-flavour corn puffs: 83 calories
- 1 slice of garlic bread: 95 calories
- 1 pot of fat-free probiotic yogurt drink and 1 apple (100 g/3½ oz): 78 calories
- 5 small strawberries topped with 2 rounded tablespoons (60 g/2½ oz) of 0% Greek yogurt with honey: 83 calories
- 1 fish finger with a serving of ketchup: 80 calories
- 1 mini Gouda-type cheese: 61 calories
- 2 cream crackers spread with 1 tablespoon of squeezy guacamole: 84 calories
- 40 g (1½ oz) rocket dressed with 2 tablespoons of low-fat balsamic dressing and 10 g (⅓ oz) grated Parmesan cheese: 71 calories
- 45 g (1½ oz) (¼ deli pot) marinated olives: 85 calories
- 1 pack of salt and vinegar mini rye crispbreads: 90 calories
- 2 clementines and 1 kiwifruit: 73 calories
- Half a slice of toast soldiers dipped into 50 g (2 oz) mild salsa from a jar: 66 calories
- 1 hard-boiled egg: 84 calories
- 60 g (2½ oz) (½ deli pot) sun-dried tomatoes in oil, drained, on a bed of salad leaves: 87 calories
- 30 g (1 oz) unshelled pistachio nuts: 86 calories
- 1 medium orange: 59 calories

- 25 g (1 oz) piece of Edam cheese: 85 calories
- 1 digestive biscuit: 71 calories
- 300 g (10 oz) shop-bought fresh carrot and coriander soup: 89 calories
- 40 g (1½ oz) canned tuna in water mashed with 30 g (1 oz) canned sweetcorn and 1 teaspoon of reduced-fat mayonnaise: 92 calories
- 1 shop-bought lemon and raisin pancake: 88 calories

50 snacks up to 50 calories

- ½ cup (80 g/3 oz) mango cubes: 46 calories
- 1 teaspoon of peanut butter spread on a celery stick: 42 calories
- 1 slice of cantaloupe melon: 23 calories
- 100 g (3½ oz) frozen summer berries with sweetener: 30 calories
- 80 g (3 oz) apple and grape snack pack: 45 calories
- 3 seafood sticks: 50 calories
- 2 clementines: 44 calories
- 80 g (3 oz) crunchy whole carrot: 28 calories
- 1 small apple: 42 calories (100 g/3½ oz weighed whole)
- 24 g (1 oz) dried apricots: 38 calories
- 100 g (3½ oz) fresh blackberries: 25 calories
- 60 g (2½ oz) fresh unpitted cherries: 23 calories
- 50 g (2 oz) cooked jumbo prawns with a squeeze of lemon: 42 calories
- 1 ginger nut biscuit: 47 calories
- 1 mini light Gouda-type cheese: 42 calories
- 2 slices of wafer-thin ham wrapped round a celery stick: 43 calories
- 1 rich tea biscuit: 38 calories
- 1 oatcake spread with yeast extract: 37 calories
- 100 g (3½ oz) cucumber with 50 g (2 oz) salsa from a jar: 26 calories
- 50 g (2 oz) red seedless grapes: 30 calories
- 100 g (3½ oz) cherry tomatoes: 20 calories
- 2 party-sized chicken satay skewers: 36 calories
- 30 g (1 oz) garlic and herb light soft cheese with celery sticks: 48 calories

- 1 sachet of miso soup with tofu: 30 calories
- 1 small (50 g/2 oz) pot of fruit-flavoured fromage frais: 49 calories
- 1 rounded tablespoon (30 g/1 oz) of shop-bought vegetable couscous salad: 48 calories
- Half a slice of Danish wholemeal toast spread with 2 teaspoons of salmon paste: 45 calories
- 2 fresh apricots: 33 calories
- 1 cream cracker topped with 10 g (⅓ oz) French chèvre: 65 calories
- 2 Melba toasts spread with 1 level teaspoon of reduced-sugar jam: 34 calories
- 100 g (3½ oz) asparagus spears, steamed, with a shake of chilli flakes: 28 calories
- 2 tablespoons of squeezy guacamole with celery sticks: 32 calories
- ½ medium banana: 47 calories
- 50 g (2 oz) (about 1 heaped tablespoon) ready-to-eat strawberry custard: 50 calories
- 1 cocktail sausage: 26 calories
- 1 bite-sized mini savoury egg: 36 calories
- 1 regular cheese triangle: 43 calories
- 40 g (1½ oz) bistro salad (lamb's lettuce, beetroot and chard) from a bag with 15 g (½ oz) pitted black olives and 1 tablespoon of low-fat French dressing: 41 calories
- 2 Cheddar cheese biscuits: 44 calories
- 1 nectarine: 45 calories
- ½ pink grapefruit, with sweetener if liked: 24 calories
- 1 cheese oatcake: 39 calories
- ½ red or orange pepper, cut into strips: 26 calories
- 2 teaspoons of toasted sunflower seeds: 42 calories
- 1 jumbo cheese-flavoured rice and corn cake: 38 calories
- 6 slices (30 g/1 oz) of bresaola: 48 calories
- 20 g (¾ oz) (2 dessertspoons) pickle with carrot sticks: 48 calories
- 1 mini pork salami sausage: 38 calories
- 2 prunes: 39 calories
- 100 g (3½ oz) ripe papaya flesh: 43 calories

Recipes

Some of the recipes in this book are for just one person, while others serve two, four or more. If you are the only one doing 5:2 in your household, you may naturally gravitate more to the ones that are single servings. However, from the feedback we've had, many couples are doing intermittent fasting together and so will love to find recipes that serve two. We've also included recipes that, despite being low calorie, taste delicious and work well for all the family or a group of adults. If you are the chief cook, not having to make a separate dish for yourself can help both practically and psychologically toward your 5:2 success. Needless to say, it is important to always only serve yourself the correct amount, and not to go back for seconds! Any of the recipes in this book can also easily be modified by multiplying or dividing ingredients as appropriate – for example doubling the ingredients to make a 'for one' recipe suitable for a couple, or halving or dividing the ingredients of a recipe for four to make it suitable for two or one. Alternatively most leftovers will keep safely in the fridge for at least 48 hours.

Fruity summer milkshake

89
CALORIES
PER SERVING

SERVES
1

- ½ ripe peach, halved, stoned and chopped
- 75 g (3 oz) strawberries, hulled
- 75 g (3 oz) raspberries
- 100 ml (3½ fl oz) milk
- ice cubes, to serve

Place the peach, strawberries and raspberries in a blender or food processor and blend to a smooth purée, scraping the mixture down from the sides of the bowl if necessary.

Add the milk and blend the ingredients again until the mixture is smooth and frothy. Pour the milkshake over the ice cubes in 2 tall glasses. Serve immediately.

Cranberry yogurt smoothie

PREPARATION TIME **3–4 MINUTES**

113
CALORIES
PER SERVING

SERVES
2

- 250 g (8 oz) apples
- 100 g (3½ oz) frozen cranberries
- 100 ml (3½ fl oz) low fat natural yogurt
- 1 tablespoon clear honey
- ice cubes, to serve

Juice the apples, then place the juice in a blender or food processor with the remaining ingredients and blend until smooth. Pour the smoothie over ice cubes in tumblers. Serve immediately.

Prune & banana crunch

274
CALORIES
PER SERVING

SERVES
2

- 1 firm, ripe banana, diced
- 100 g (3½ oz) ready-to-eat pitted prunes
- 250 g (8 oz) 0% Greek yogurt
- 40 g (1½ oz) cornflakes or crunchy cereal flakes

Mix together the banana, prunes and yogurt in a large bowl.

Spoon into 2 glass serving bowls and top with the cornflakes or crunchy cereal flakes. Serve immediately.

Spiced apple porridge

174
CALORIES
PER SERVING

SERVES
1

- 225 ml (7½ fl oz) apple juice
- ½ teaspoon ground cinnamon
- 25 g (1 oz) millet flakes

To serve
- 1 tablespoon 0% fat Greek yogurt
- demerara sugar (optional)

Put the apple juice and cinnamon in a microwaveable serving bowl. Sprinkle in the millet flakes and stir gently.

Microwave on full power for 3–4 minutes, stirring frequently, until thick and creamy. Alternatively, put the ingredients in a small saucepan and heat gently for 6–8 minutes, stirring frequently, until thick and creamy. Add a little extra juice if the mixture becomes dry. Serve hot with a tablespoon of yogurt and, if you like your porridge sweet, a teaspoon of sugar (remembering to count the calories).

Apple & yogurt muesli

PREPARATION TIME **10 MINUTES, PLUS SOAKING**

 303 CALORIES PER SERVING

 SERVES **2**

- 75 g (3 oz) fruit and nut muesli, preferably no-added-sugar
- 1 dessert apple, such as Granny Smiths, peeled and coarsely grated
- 200 ml (⅓ pint) chilled apple juice
- 125 g (4 oz) 0% Greek yogurt with honey

To serve
- linseeds (optional)
- runny honey (optional)

Put the muesli in a bowl and mix with the apples. Pour over the apple juice, stir well to combine and leave to soak for 5–6 minutes.

Divide the soaked muesli among 2 serving bowls and spoon the yogurt on top. Scatter over the linseeds, if using, and serve with a drizzle of honey, if liked (remembering to count the calories).

Maple-glazed granola

246 CALORIES PER SERVING

SERVES **3**

- 1 tablespoon olive oil
- 1 tablespoon maple syrup
- 20 g (¾ oz) flaked almonds
- 20 g (¾ oz) pine nuts
- 15 g (½ oz) sunflower seeds
- 15 g (½ oz) porridge oats
- 175 g (6 oz) natural yogurt

Fruit salad
- ½ mango, peeled, stoned and sliced
- 1 kiwifruit, peeled and sliced
- handful of red seedless grapes, halved
- grated rind and juice of ½ lime

Heat the oil in a flameproof frying pan with a metal handle, add the maple syrup and the nuts, seeds and oats and toss together.

Transfer the pan to a preheated oven, 180°C (350°F), Gas Mark 4, and cook for 5–8 minutes, stirring once and moving the brown edges to the centre, until the granola mixture is evenly toasted. Leave to cool. (The cooled granola can be stored in a sealed jar for up to 10 days.)

To make the fruit salad, mix together the fruits and lime rind and juice in a bowl, then divide among 3 dishes. Spoon the yogurt on top, sprinkle over the granola and serve.

TOP TIP

Make a list of the reasons why you are fasting and stick it on front of your fridge. This will remind you of your goals whenever you reach for something to eat!

Blueberry bran muffins

142 CALORIES PER SERVING

SERVES 12

250 g (8 oz) plain flour
50 g (2 oz) bran
1 teaspoon baking powder
1 teaspoon bicarbonate
soda
3 eggs
1 teaspoon vanilla extract
250 ml (8 fl oz) buttermilk
50 ml (2 fl oz) rice bran,
groundnut or sunflower
oil, plus extra for greasing
125 g (4 oz) blueberries

Mix together the dry ingredients in a large bowl until well combined. Lightly beat the eggs in a large jug, then stir in the vanilla extract, buttermilk and oil.

Pour the wet ingredients into the dry ingredients, then add the blueberries and fold in gently using a large metal spoon until only just combined.

Using a spring-back ice-cream scoop or large metal spoon, divide the mixture among the sections of a lightly oiled or paper-case-lined 12-hole muffin tin.

Bake in a preheated oven, 180°C (350°F), Gas Mark 4, for 18–20 minutes until risen, golden and firm. Transfer to a wire rack to cool slightly before serving warm.

Cranberry muffins

PREPARATION TIME **10 MINUTES** • COOKING TIME **18–20 MINUTES**

172 CALORIES PER SERVING **SERVES 12**

- 150 g (5 oz) plain flour
- 150 g (5 oz) self-raising flour
- 1 tablespoon baking powder
- 65 g (2½ oz) light muscovado sugar
- 3 pieces of stem ginger from a jar, about 50 g (2 oz), finely chopped
- 100 g (3½ oz) dried cranberries
- 1 egg
- 250 ml (8 fl oz) milk
- 4 tablespoons vegetable oil

Sift the flours and baking powder into a large bowl, then stir in the sugar, ginger and cranberries until well combined. Beat together the egg, milk and oil in a jug.

Pour the wet ingredients into the dry ingredients, then stir gently using a large metal spoon until only just combined. The mixture should look craggy, with specks of flour still visible.

Using a spring-back ice-cream scoop or large metal spoon, divide the mixture among the sections of a paper-case-lined 12-hole muffin tin, piling it up in the centres.

Bake in a preheated oven, 200°C (400°F), Gas Mark 6, for 18–20 minutes, until well risen and golden. Transfer to a wire rack to cool slightly before serving warm.

Pistachio & date squares

PREPARATION TIME **10 MINUTES, PLUS COOLING AND CHILLING** • COOKING TIME **20 MINUTES**

171 CALORIES PER SERVING

SERVES **20**

grated rind of 1 lemon

75 g (3 oz) ready-to-eat dried dates, chopped

75 g (3 oz) unsalted pistachio nuts, chopped

75 g (3 oz) flaked almonds, chopped

125 g (4 oz) soft light brown sugar

150 g (5 oz) millet flakes

40 g (1½ oz) cornflakes, lightly crushed

400 g (13 oz) can condensed milk

25 g (1 oz) mixed seeds, such as pumpkin and sunflower

Mix together all the ingredients in a large bowl, then spoon into a 28 x 18 cm (11 x 7 inch) baking tin and spread evenly.

Place in a preheated oven, 180°C (350°F), Gas Mark 4, for 20 minutes. Leave to cool in the tin, then mark into 20 squares and chill until firm.

TOP TIP

To prepare for your fast day, shop in advance for all the ingredients you will need and try to make sure that there are no tempting snacks on hand that might lead you astray.

Moroccan baked eggs

PREPARATION TIME **10 MINUTES** • COOKING TIME **25–35 MINUTES**

170 CALORIES PER SERVING

SERVES 2

- ½ tablespoon olive oil
- ½ onion, chopped
- 1 garlic clove, sliced
- ½ teaspoon ras el hanout
- pinch ground cinnamon
- ½ teaspoon ground coriander
- 400 g (13 oz) cherry tomatoes
- 2 tablespoons chopped coriander
- 2 eggs
- salt and pepper

Heat the oil in a frying pan over a medium heat, add the onion and garlic and cook for 6–7 minutes or until softened and lightly golden, stirring occasionally. Stir in the spices and cook for a further 1 minute. Add the tomatoes and season well with salt and pepper, then simmer gently for 8–10 minutes.

Scatter over 3 teaspoons of the coriander, then divide the tomato mixture among 2 individual ovenproof dishes. Break an egg into each dish.

Bake in a preheated oven, 220°C (425°F), Gas Mark 7, for 8–10 minutes until the egg is set but the yolks are still slightly runny. Cook for a further 2–3 minutes if you prefer the eggs to be cooked through. Serve scattered with the remaining coriander.

Ham & tomato omelettes

PREPARATION TIME **20 MINUTES** • COOKING TIME **30 MINUTES**

278 CALORIES PER SERVING

SERVES 4

- 4 teaspoons extra virgin rapeseed oil
- 4 shallots, thinly sliced
- 8 eggs, lightly beaten
- 2 tablespoons chopped fresh mixed herbs, such as chives, chervil, parsley, basil and thyme
- 200 g (7 oz) yellow and red cherry tomatoes, halved
- 150 g (5 oz) wafer-thin smoked ham slices
- salt and pepper

Heat 1 teaspoon of the oil in a medium-sized frying pan over a medium-low heat, add the shallots and cook gently for 4–5 minutes or until softened.

Meanwhile, beat together the eggs and herbs in a large jug and season with salt and pepper.

Remove three-quarters of the shallots from the pan with a slotted spoon and set aside. Pour one-quarter of the egg mixture into the pan, then scatter over one-quarter of the cherry tomatoes and stir gently, using a heat-resistant rubber spatula, until the egg is almost set. Scatter one-quarter of the sliced ham evenly over the top of the omelette and cook gently for a further 1 minute.

Fold the omelette in half, slide out of the pan on to a warm plate and serve immediately. Repeat with the remaining ingredients to make 3 more omelettes. Alternatively, keep the cooked omelettes warm until all 4 are ready and serve at the same time.

Red pepper & ginger soup

PREPARATION TIME **20 MINUTES, PLUS COOLING** • COOKING TIME **45 MINUTES**

112 CALORIES PER SERVING

SERVES 2

- 1½ red peppers, quartered, cored and deseeded
- ½ red onion, quartered
- 1 garlic clove, unpeeled
- ½ teaspoon olive oil
- 2.5 cm (1 inch) piece of fresh root ginger, peeled and grated
- ½ teaspoon ground cumin
- ½ teaspoon ground coriander
- 1 medium potato, peeled and chopped
- 450 ml (¾ pint) vegetable stock
- salt and pepper
- 2 tablespoons low-fat fromage frais, to serve

Place the peppers, onion and garlic in a nonstick roasting tin. Roast in a preheated oven, 200°C (400°F), Gas Mark 6, for 40 minutes or until the peppers have blistered and the onion and garlic are soft. If the onion quarters start to brown too much, cover them with the pepper halves.

Meanwhile, heat the oil in a saucepan, add the ginger, cumin and coriander and fry over a low heat for 1–2 minutes or until softened. Add the potato, stir well and season with salt and pepper, then pour in the stock. Cover and simmer for 30 minutes.

Remove the vegetables from the oven. Place the peppers in a plastic bag, tie the top and leave to cool. (The steam produced in the bag makes it easier to remove the skin when the peppers are cool.) Add the onions to the potato mixture and carefully squeeze out the garlic pulp into the saucepan. Peel the peppers and add all but one quarter to the soup. Simmer for 5 minutes.

Transfer the soup to a blender or food processor and blend until smooth. Alternatively, rub the soup through a sieve to purée. Return the soup to the pan and thin with a little water, if necessary. Heat through gently.

Slice the remaining pepper. Ladle the soup into 2 warm bowls and arrange pepper slices on top of each with a spoonful of fromage frais.

Ginger & parsnip soup

PREPARATION TIME **10 MINUTES** • COOKING TIME **20 MINUTES**

151 CALORIES PER SERVING SERVES **2**

- 15 g (½ oz) butter
- 25 g (1 oz) fresh root ginger, peeled and thinly sliced
- ½ bunch of spring onions
- 250 g (8 oz) parsnips, peeled and sliced
- 600 ml (1 pint) vegetable stock
- salt and pepper

Melt the butter in a saucepan, add the ginger and fry gently for 1 minute. Reserve ½ a spring onion. Roughly chop the remainder and add to the pan with the parsnips. Fry gently for 2 minutes.

Add the stock and bring to the boil. Reduce the heat, cover and simmer gently for 15 minutes until the parsnips are tender.

Meanwhile, shred the reserved spring onion lengthways into fine ribbons.

Transfer the soup to a blender or food processor and blend until smooth. Alternatively, blend in the pan using a hand-held electric blender. Return the soup to the pan, if necessary, season with salt and pepper and heat through gently for 1 minute. Serve the soup scattered with the spring onion ribbons.

Coconut & butternut soup

PREPARATION TIME **10 MINUTES** • COOKING TIME **25 MINUTES**

120
CALORIES
PER SERVING

SERVES
6

- 1 tablespoon olive oil
- 1 onion, chopped
- 1 garlic clove, crushed
- 2 butternut squashes, peeled, deseeded and cubed
- 2 teaspoons medium curry paste
- 600 ml (1 pint) vegetable stock
- 200 ml (7 fl oz) reduced-fat coconut milk
- 2 tablespoons chopped coriander

Heat the oil in a large saucepan, add the onion and garlic and fry for 4–5 minutes until softened. Add the squash and fry for 1 minute, then stir in the curry paste and fry for a further 1 minute.

Pour in the stock and bring to the boil, then reduce the heat, cover and simmer for 15 minutes until the squash is tender.

Transfer the soup to a blender or food processor and blend until smooth. Return the soup to the pan, stir in the coconut milk and coriander and season with salt and pepper. Heat through gently before serving.

Quick & easy miso soup

PREPARATION TIME **5 MINUTES** • COOKING TIME **10 MINUTES**

58
CALORIES
PER SERVING

SERVES
2

- 450 ml (¾ pints) vegetable stock
- 1 tablespoon miso paste
- 50 g (2 oz) shiitake mushrooms, sliced
- 125 g (4 oz) tofu, cubed

Pour the stock into a saucepan and heat until simmering.

Add the miso paste, shiitake mushrooms and tofu to the stock and simmer for 5 minutes. Ladle the soup into 2 warm bowls and serve.

Hot & sour mushroom soup

PREPARATION TIME **5 MINUTES** • COOKING TIME **15 MINUTES**

23 CALORIES PER SERVING

SERVES 4

- 1.2 litres (2 pints) fish stock
- 1 lemon grass stalk, lightly crushed
- 3 fresh kaffir lime leaves or 3 pieces of lime rind
- 2 Thai red chillies, halved and deseeded
- 2 tablespoons lime juice
- 2 tablespoons Thai fish sauce
- 50 g (2 oz) can bamboo shoots
- 125 g (4 oz) oyster mushrooms
- 2 spring onions, finely sliced
- ½ red chilli, sliced, to garnish

Pour the stock into a saucepan and add the lemon grass, lime leaves or rind and chillies. Simmer for 10 minutes.

Strain the liquid into a clean saucepan. Reserve a little red chilli and discard the remaining seasonings. Add the lime juice and fish sauce to the soup with the bamboo shoots and mushrooms and reserved chilli.

Simmer the soup for 5 minutes, then ladle into 4 warm bowls and sprinkle with the spring onions. Serve garnished with red chilli slices.

Hot & sour prawn soup

PREPARATION TIME **10 MINUTES** • COOKING TIME **20 MINUTES**

282 CALORIES PER SERVING

SERVES **4**

1 litre (1¾ pints) light and clear chicken or vegetable stock
3 tablespoons Thai fish sauce
1 tablespoon rice wine vinegar
1 tablespoon lime juice
1 tablespoon palm sugar or soft light brown sugar
1 garlic clove, sliced
1 red chilli, thinly sliced
3 kaffir lime leaves
2 teaspoons tamarind paste
200 g (7 oz) rice vermicelli
125 g (4 oz) baby corn, sliced
250 g (8 oz) raw peeled tiger prawns
100 g (3½ oz) bean sprouts
2 tablespoons shredded mint

Pour the stock into a large saucepan and add the fish sauce, vinegar, lime juice, sugar, garlic, chilli, lime leaves and tamarind paste. Bring to the boil over a medium-high heat, then reduce the heat and simmer gently for 12 minutes.

Meanwhile, put the rice vermicelli in a bowl of boiling water and leave to stand for 2–3 minutes until tender, or cook according to the packet instructions. Drain well and divide among 4 warm deep serving bowls.

Stir the baby corn into the broth and simmer for 2 minutes, then add the prawns and simmer for a further 2–3 minutes until the prawns turn pink and are just cooked through.

Ladle the broth over the vermicelli, then scatter over the bean sprouts and mint and serve immediately.

Fragrant soba noodle soup

PREPARATION TIME **10 MINUTES** • COOKING TIME **12–14 MINUTES**

314 CALORIES PER SERVING · **SERVES 4**

- 1.2 litres (2 pints) clear chicken or vegetable stock
- 1 lemon grass stalk, finely sliced
- 2.5 cm (1 inch) piece of fresh root ginger, peeled and finely chopped
- 3 lime leaves, thinly sliced
- 1 small red chilli, deseeded and finely sliced (optional)
- 1 tablespoon fish sauce
- 250 g (8 oz) buckwheat soba noodles
- 200 g (7 oz) firm tofu, diced
- 1 spring onion, thinly sliced
- 2 tablespoons chopped coriander

Pour the stock into a saucepan and add the lemon grass, ginger, lime leaves, chilli, if using, and fish sauce. Bring to the boil, then reduce the heat to low and simmer gently for 10–12 minutes.

Meanwhile, bring a large saucepan of water to the boil and cook the noodles for 6–7 minutes, or according to the packet instructions, until tender. Drain the noodles and divide among 4 warm serving bowls.

Scatter the tofu over the noodles and then carefully ladle over the hot soup. Scatter over the spring onion and coriander and serve immediately.

Butternut & rosemary soup

146 CALORIES PER SERVING

SERVES 4

- 1 butternut squash, halved, deseeded and cut into small chunks
- a few rosemary sprigs, plus extra leaves to garnish
- 150 g (5 oz) red lentils, washed and drained
- 1 onion, finely chopped
- 900 ml (1½ pints) vegetable stock
- salt and pepper

Place the squash pieces in a nonstick roasting tin. Sprinkle over the rosemary and season with salt and pepper. Roast in a preheated oven, 200°C (400°F), Gas Mark 6, for 45 minutes.

Meanwhile, put the lentils in a saucepan and cover with water, then bring to the boil and boil rapidly for 10 minutes. Drain, then return to a clean saucepan with the onion and stock and simmer for 5 minutes. Season with salt and pepper.

Remove the squash from the oven and scoop the flesh from the skin. Mash the flesh with a fork and add it to the soup, then simmer for 25 minutes until the lentils are tender. Serve the soup scattered with extra rosemary.

Lentil & goats' cheese salad

PREPARATION TIME **10 MINUTES** • COOKING TIME **20–30 MINUTE**

250 CALORIES PER SERVING

SERVES 2

- 1 teaspoon olive oil
- 1 teaspoon cumin seeds
- 1 garlic clove, crushed
- 1 teaspoon peeled and grated fresh root ginger
- 50 g (2 oz) Puy lentils
- 375 ml (13 fl oz) hot chicken or vegetable stock
- 1 tablespoon chopped mint
- 1 tablespoon chopped coriander
- squeeze of lime juice
- 75 g (3 oz) baby spinach leaves
- 50 g (2 oz) goats' cheese, crumbled
- pepper

Heat the oil in a saucepan over a medium heat, add the cumin seeds, garlic and ginger and cook for 1 minute. Add the lentils and cook for a further 1 minute.

Pour the stock into the pan one ladleful at a time, waiting until the liquid has been absorbed before adding more, and cook until the lentils are tender – about 10-20 minutes. Remove the pan from the heat and stir in the herbs and lime juice.

Divide the spinach leaves among 2 serving bowls, top with the lentils and goats' cheese and sprinkle with black pepper.

TOP TIP

Watch out for condiments. Replace ketchup, mayonnaise or salad dressing with balsamic vinegar, mustard or lemon juice, which have fewer calories.

Vietnamese-style noodle salad

PREPARATION TIME **20 MINUTES** • COOKING TIME **4 MINUTES**

271 CALORIES PER SERVING

SERVES **4**

- 200 g (7 oz) fine rice noodles
- ½ cucumber, deseeded and cut into matchsticks
- 1 carrot, cut into matchsticks
- 150 g (5 oz) bean sprouts
- 125 g (4 oz) mangetout, cut into thin strips
- 2 tablespoons chopped coriander
- 2 tablespoons chopped mint
- 1 red chilli, deseeded and finely sliced
- 2 tablespoons chopped blanched peanuts, to garnish

Dressing
- 1 tablespoon sunflower or groundnut oil
- ½ teaspoon caster sugar
- 1 tablespoon fish sauce
- 2 tablespoons lime juice

Bring a large saucepan of water to the boil, then turn off the heat and add the rice noodles. Cover and leave to cook for 4 minutes, or according to the packet instructions, until just tender. Drain the noodles and cool immediately in a bowl of ice-cold water.

Make the dressing by combining all the ingredients in a screw-top jar until the sugar is dissolved.

Drain the noodles and return to the bowl. Pour over half of the dressing, then tip in the vegetables, herbs and chilli. Toss until well combined.

Heap the noodle salad on 4 serving plates and drizzle with the remaining dressing. Serve scattered with the chopped peanuts.

Spiced chicken & mango salad

PREPARATION TIME **15 MINUTES** • COOKING TIME **5–6 MINUTES**

221 CALORIES PER SERVING

SERVES 2

3 teaspoons mild curry paste
juice of ½ lemon
2 small boneless, skinless chicken breasts, cut into long, thin strips
75 g (3 oz) low-fat natural yogurt
25 g (1 oz) watercress, torn into pieces
¼ cucumber, diced
¼ red onion, chopped
½ mango, peeled, stoned and cut into chunks
¼ iceberg lettuce, torn into pieces

Put 2 teaspoons of the curry paste in a plastic bag with the lemon juice and mix together by squeezing the bag. Add the chicken and toss together.

Arrange the chicken in a single layer in a steamer set over a large saucepan of boiling water, cover and cook for 5–6 minutes or until cooked through.

Meanwhile, mix the remaining curry paste in a bowl with the yogurt. Add the watercress to the yogurt dressing with the cucumber, red onion and mango and gently toss together.

Divide the lettuce among 2 serving plates, spoon over the mango mixture and top with the warm chicken strips. Serve immediately.

Griddled chicken salad

PREPARATION TIME **10 MINUTES** • COOKING TIME **10 MINUTES**

298 CALORIES PER SERVING

SERVES **2**

- 2 chicken breast fillets, about 125 g/4 oz per chicken breast
- ½ tablespoon olive oil
- 50 g (2 oz) cooked pearl barley
- ½ red onion, finely chopped
- ½ red chilli, finely chopped
- 2 tablespoons chopped coriander
- grated rind and juice of 1 lime
- ½ red pepper, cored, deseeded and finely chopped
- salt and pepper
- parsley sprigs, to garnish
- lime wedges, to serve

Brush each chicken breast with a little oil. Heat a griddle pan until hot, add the chicken and cook for 4–5 minutes on each side or until cooked through and browned. Cut each breast into 4 slices.

Put the barley in a large bowl and stir in the remaining oil. Add the remaining ingredients, season with salt and pepper and stir to combine.

Spoon the barley on to 2 serving plates, top with the griddled chicken and garnish with sprigs of parsley. Serve with lime wedges.

TOP TIP

It's possible to confuse hunger with thirst so, when you feel hungry, try drinking a large glass of water. To stay healthy and hydrated throughout the day it is important to drink plenty of water.

Italian broccoli & egg salad

PREPARATION TIME **10 MINUTES** • COOKING TIME **5 MINUTES**

198 CALORIES PER SERVING

SERVES 2

150 g (5 oz) broccoli
1 small leek, about 150 g
(5 oz) in total, trimmed
and thickly sliced
2 hard-boiled eggs

Dressing
2 tablespoons lemon juice
1 tablespoon olive oil
1 teaspoon clear honey
½ tablespoon capers, well
drained
1 tablespoons chopped
tarragon, plus extra sprigs
to garnish (optional)
salt and pepper

Cut the broccoli into florets and thickly slice the stems.
Put the broccoli in a steamer set over a saucepan of boiling
water, cover and cook for 3 minutes, then add the leeks and
cook for a further 2 minutes.

Meanwhile, make the dressing by combining all the
ingredients in a salad bowl, then season with salt and pepper.

Shell and roughly chop the eggs.

Add the broccoli and leeks to the dressing, toss together and
sprinkle with the chopped eggs. Garnish with tarragon sprigs,
if liked, and serve warm.

Shiitake mushroom omelette

PREPARATION TIME **5 MINUTES** • COOKING TIME **5 MINUTES**

270 CALORIES PER SERVING

SERVES **2**

- 2 teaspoons sesame oil
- 125 g (4 oz) shiitake mushrooms, sliced
- 3 tablespoons chopped chives, plus extra to garnish
- 1 teaspoon miso paste
- 50 ml (2 fl oz) boiling water
- 5 eggs, lightly beaten
- pepper

Heat the oil in a frying pan over a medium heat, add the mushrooms and chives and stir-fry for 2 minutes.

Dissolve the miso in the boiling water and add to the pan. Continue to fry until the liquid has evaporated.

Pour the eggs over the mushroom mixture and swirl around the pan to form a thin omelette. Cook for 1 minute.

Remove the omelette from the heat and slide on to a plate. Roll up and sprinkle with pepper and a few extra chives. Cut in half, place on 2 serving plates and serve hot.

TOP TIP

Keep a record of everything you eat and drink in a food journal. This is a good way to make sure that you are staying within you calorie limit while still eating a balanced diet.

Baked field mushrooms

PREPARATION TIME **10 MINUTES** • COOKING TIME **40 MINUTES**

42 CALORIES PER SERVING

SERVES **2**

- 2½ large field or open cap mushrooms
- 2 tablespoons balsamic vinegar
- ½ tablespoon wholegrain mustard
- 40 g (1½ oz) watercress
- salt and pepper
- Parmesan cheese shavings, to serve (optional)

Remove and reserve the stalks from 2 of the mushrooms. Place the 2 mushrooms, skin side down, in a small nonstick roasting tin and bake in a preheated oven, 200°C (400°F), Gas Mark 6, for 15 minutes.

Meanwhile, make the dressing. Finely chop the remaining half mushroom and the reserved stalks and mix them in a small bowl with the vinegar and mustard. Season with salt and pepper.

Remove the mushrooms from the oven and spoon some dressing over each one. Return to the oven and cook for a further 25 minutes, covering the tin with foil after 10 minutes.

Transfer the mushrooms to a plate and keep warm. Tip the watercress into the hot juices and toss well. Spoon piles of watercress on to 2 serving plates. Place a mushroom on each and sprinkle with Parmesan shavings, if using.

Mushroom crêpes

PREPARATION TIME **20–25 MINUTES** • COOKING TIME **35 MINUTES**

112 CALORIES PER SERVING · **SERVES 4**

- 50 g (2 oz) plain flour
- 150 ml (¼ pint) skimmed milk
- 1 small egg, beaten
- 1 teaspoon olive oil
- salt and pepper
- flat leaf parsley sprigs, to garnish

Filling
- 300 g (10 oz) chestnut mushrooms, chopped
- 1 bunch of spring onions, finely chopped
- 1 garlic clove, chopped
- 400 g (13 oz) can chopped tomatoes, drained
- 2 tablespoons chopped oregano

Place the flour, milk, egg and salt and pepper in a blender or food processor and blend until smooth or whisk by hand.

Heat a few drops of oil in a nonstick frying pan. Pour in a ladleful of the batter and cook for 1 minute. Carefully flip the pancake over and cook the other side. Slide the pancake out of the pan on to greaseproof paper. Make 3 more pancakes in the same way, adding a few more drops of oil to the pan between each one, and stack the pancakes between sheets of greaseproof paper.

Meanwhile, make the filling. Put all the ingredients in a small saucepan and cook for 5 minutes, stirring occasionally. Divide the filling among the pancakes, reserving a little of the mixture to serve, then roll them up.

Transfer the pancakes to an ovenproof dish and place in a preheated oven, 180°C (350°F), Gas Mark 4, for 20 minutes. Serve with the remaining mushroom mixture and garnish with parsley sprigs.

Basil & tomato ste

228 CALORIES PER SERVING

SERVES 4

- 1 kg (2 lb) ripe tomatoes
- 6 tablespoons olive oil
- 2 onions, chopped
- 4 celery sticks, sliced
- 4 plump garlic cloves, thinly sliced
- 175 g (6 oz) mushrooms, sliced
- 3 tablespoons sun-dried tomato paste
- 600 ml (1 pint) vegetable stock
- 1 tablespoon muscovado sugar
- 3 tablespoons capers, drained
- large handful of basil leaves, about 15 g (½ oz), torn
- large handful of chervil or flat leaf parsley, about 15 g (½ oz), torn
- salt and pepper

Put the tomatoes in a large saucepan or heatproof bowl a pour over enough boiling water to cover, then leave for abo 1 minute. Drain, then skin the tomatoes carefully. Quarter and deseed the tomatoes, scooping out the pulp into a sieve over a bowl to catch the juices.

Heat 4 tablespoons of the oil in a large saucepan, add the onions and celery and fry for 5 minutes. Add the garlic and mushrooms and fry for a further 3 minutes.

Add the tomatoes and their juices, the sun-dried tomato paste, stock, sugar and capers and bring to the boil. Reduce the heat and simmer gently, uncovered, for 5 minutes.

Add the herbs to the pan with a little salt and pepper and cook for 1 minute. Ladle into 4 serving bowls, drizzle with the remaining oil and serve.

ash & ricotta frittata

- 1 tablespoon extra virgin rapeseed oil
- 1 red onion, thinly sliced
- 450 g (14½ oz) peeled butternut squash, diced
- 8 eggs
- 1 tablespoon chopped thyme
- 2 tablespoons chopped sage
- 125 g (4 oz) ricotta cheese
- salt and pepper

Heat the oil in a large, deep frying pan with an ovenproof handle over a medium-low heat, add the onion and butternut squash, then cover loosely and cook gently, stirring frequently, for 18–20 minutes or until softened and golden.

Lightly beat the eggs, thyme, sage and ricotta in a jug, then season well with salt and pepper and pour over the butternut squash.

Cook for a further 2–3 minutes until the egg is almost set, stirring occasionally with a heat-resistant rubber spatula to prevent the base from burning.

Slide the pan under a preheated grill, keeping the handle away from the heat, and grill for 3–4 minutes or until the egg is set and the frittata is golden. Slice into 6 wedges and serve hot.

Leek & tomato filo tarts

PREPARATION TIME **20 MINUTES, PLUS SOAKING** • COOKING TIME **30 MINUTES**

135 CALORIES PER SERVING

SERVES 4

- 8 sun-dried tomatoes
- 2 leeks, trimmed and thinly sliced
- 300 ml (½ pint) white wine
- 2 tablespoons skimmed milk
- 1 small egg, separated
- 50 g (2 oz) low-fat soft cheese
- 12 pieces of filo pastry, each about 15 cm (6 inches) square
- salt and pepper

Put the tomatoes in a small bowl and pour over enough boiling water to cover. Leave to soak for 20 minutes.

Meanwhile, put the leeks and wine in a saucepan and bring to the boil, then reduce the heat and simmer until the liquid has evaporated. Remove the pan from the heat and stir in the milk, egg yolk and cheese. Season with salt and pepper.

Brush a pastry square with a little egg white and use it to line the base and sides of a 10 cm (4 inch) tart tin. Brush 2 more squares and lay these on top, each at a slight angle to the first, allowing the edges to flop over the rim. Repeat with the remaining squares to line 3 more tart tins.

Put a spoonful of the cooked leek mixture in each pastry case. Lay 2 of the rehydrated tomatoes on top of each tart and cover with the remaining leek mixture. Season again and place in a preheated oven, 200°C (400°F), Gas Mark 6, for 20 minutes, covering the tarts with pieces of foil after 10 minutes. Serve hot.

Red lentil dhal with okra

PREPARATION TIME **5 MINUTES** • COOKING TIME **20 MINUTES**

366 CALORIES PER SERVING

SERVES **4**

- 1 onion, chopped
- 250 g (8 oz) red lentils, washed and drained
- 1 teaspoon ground turmeric
- 1 green chilli, deseeded and sliced
- 2 tablespoons tomato purée
- 900 ml (1½ pints) vegetable stock
- 25 g (1 oz) creamed coconut
- 2 tablespoons groundnut or vegetable oil
- 250 g (8 oz) okra, trimmed and halved crossways
- 2 teaspoons cumin seeds
- 1 tablespoon mustard seeds
- 2 teaspoons black onion seeds
- 2 garlic cloves, chopped
- 6 curry leaves (optional)
- salt and pepper

Put the onion, lentils, turmeric, chilli, tomato purée, stock and creamed coconut in a saucepan. Bring to the boil, then reduce the heat and simmer gently, uncovered, for 15 minutes, stirring frequently, until thickened and pulpy.

Meanwhile, heat the oil in a frying pan, add the okra, cumin seeds, mustard seeds, black onion seeds, garlic and curry leaves, if using, and fry gently for about 5 minutes until the okra is tender.

Season the lentil dhal with salt and pepper and serve topped with the spiced okra.

Asparagus with smoked salmon

PREPARATION TIME **10 MINUTES** • COOKING TIME **6 MINUTES**

150 CALORIES PER SERVING

SERVES 6

- 200 g (7 oz) trimmed asparagus
- 3 tablespoons roughly chopped hazelnuts
- 4 teaspoons olive oil
- juice of 1 lime
- 1 teaspoon Dijon mustard
- 12 quail eggs
- 250 g (8 oz) smoked salmon
- salt and pepper

Put the asparagus in a steamer set over a saucepan of boiling water, cover and cook for 5 minutes until just tender.

Meanwhile, put the nuts in a foil-lined grill pan and cook under a preheated grill until lightly browned. In a bowl, lightly mix together the oil, lime juice and mustard with a little salt and pepper, then stir in the hot nuts. Keep warm.

Pour water into a saucepan to a depth of 4 cm (1½ inches) and bring it to the boil. Lower the eggs into the water with a slotted spoon and cook for 1 minute. Remove the pan from the heat and leave the eggs to stand for 1 minute. Drain the eggs, then cool under cold running water and drain again.

Tear the salmon into strips and divide among 6 serving plates. Do the same with the asparagus, then halve the quail eggs, leaving the shells on if liked, and arrange on top. Drizzle with the warm nut dressing and sprinkled with a little black pepper.

Chilli rice noodles

PREPARATION TIME **10 MINUTES** • COOKING TIME **3–4 MINUTES**

283 CALORIES PER SERVING

SERVES **2**

- 4 teaspoons seasoned rice vinegar
- 1 tablespoon caster sugar
- 1 teaspoon Thai fish sauce
- 1 tablespoon soy sauce
- 100 g (3½ oz) dried rice ribbon noodles
- 1 tablespoon vegetable or groundnut oil
- 1 small red chilli, deseeded and finely shredded
- 1 small red pepper, cored, deseeded and finely shredded
- 50 g (2 oz) mangetout, thinly sliced lengthways

Mix together the vinegar, sugar, fish sauce and soy sauce in a non-metallic bowl and set aside.

Bring a large saucepan of water to the boil, then turn off the heat and add the rice noodles. Cover and leave to cook for 3–4 minutes, or according to the packet instructions, until tender.

Meanwhile, heat the oil in a frying pan, add the chilli, red pepper and mangetout and fry for 3 minutes until softened.

Drain the noodles and add to the frying pan with the reserved sauce mixture. Toss together, then serve immediately.

TOP TIP

Find yourself a diet buddy. Dieting together can introduce a bit of healthy competition and you can encourage each other when the going gets tough.

Thai dressed rolls

PREPARATION TIME **10 MINUTES**

272 CALORIES PER SERVING

SERVES 4

1 small iceburg lettuce
275 g (9 oz) tofu, diced
100 g (3½ oz) mangetout,
shredded lengthways

Dressing
2 tablespoons sesame oil
2 tablespoons light soy
sauce
2 tablespoons lime juice
1 tablespoon muscovado
sugar
1 Thai chilli, deseeded and
sliced
1 garlic clove, crushed
pepper

Remove 8 leaves from the lettuce. Fill a large heatproof bowl with boiling water. Add the separated leaves and leave to stand for 10 seconds. Drain and refresh under cold running water, then drain again thoroughly.

Finely shred the remaining lettuce and toss in a bowl with the tofu and mangetout.

Make the dressing by combining all the ingredients in a screw-top jar. Pour over the tofu and gently toss together.

Spoon a little mixture on to the centre of each blanched lettuce leaf, then roll up. Chill until ready to serve, then divide among 4 serving plates and serve.

Lime & ginger prawn coleslaw

PREPARATION TIME **15 MINUTES** • COOKING TIME **2–3 MINUTES**

143 CALORIES PER SERVING

SERVES 2

- ¼ Chinese cabbage or pointed spring cabbage, thinly shredded
- 1 carrot, coarsely grated
- 100 g (3½ oz) bean sprouts
- ½ small bunch of coriander, finely chopped
- 1 spring onion, thinly sliced
- 125 g (4 oz) raw peeled king prawns
- 1 teaspoon Chinese 5-spice powder
- ½ tablespoon groundnut oil
- lime wedges, to serve

Dressing
- 1 teaspoon peeled and finely grated fresh root ginger
- 1 tablespoon lime juice
- ½ teaspoon palm sugar or soft light brown sugar
- 1 tablespoon light soy sauce
- ½ tablespoon groundnut oil

Toss together the cabbage, carrots, bean sprouts, coriander and spring onion in a large bowl and set aside.

Make the dressing by combining all the ingredients in a screw-top jar and set aside.

Mix together the prawns and Chinese 5-spice powder in a bowl until the prawns are well coated. Heat the oil in a wok or frying pan over a medium-high heat, add the prawns and stir-fry for 2–3 minutes or until the prawns turn pink and are cooked through. Remove from the pan and drain on kitchen paper.

Pour the dressing over the vegetables and toss together, then heap the coleslaw on 2 serving plates. Scatter over the prawns and serve with lime wedges.

Piri piri prawns

PREPARATION TIME **15 MINUTES, PLUS MARINATING** • COOKING TIME **5–6 MINUTES**

104 CALORIES PER SERVING

SERVES **6**

400 g (13 oz) raw tiger prawns, shell on with heads removed
chopped parsley, to garnish
lemon wedges, to serve

Marinade
3 tablespoons olive oil
grated rind and juice of 1 lemon
2 teaspoons piri-piri seasoning
2 teaspoons tomato purée
2 garlic cloves, finely chopped
salt and pepper

Put the prawns in a sieve, rinse under cold running water and drain well.

Mix together the marinade ingredients in a shallow non-metallic bowl. Add the prawns and toss until evenly coated. Cover and leave to marinate in the refrigerator for at least 2 hours.

Thread the prawns on to 12 metal skewers through the thickest part of the body and tail. Cook under a preheated grill for 5–6 minutes, turning once, until the prawns turn pink and are cooked through.

Serve 2 skewers per person, sprinkled with chopped parsley, with lemon wedges.

Prawn & mango kebabs

PREPARATION TIME **15 MINUTES, PLUS MARINATING** • COOKING TIME **4 MINUTES**

111 CALORIES PER SERVING

SERVES 4

- 16 raw peeled large tiger prawns
- 1 large mango, peeled, stoned and cut into 16 bite-sized pieces
- undressed salad, to serve

Marinade
- 1 tablespoon sunflower oil
- 4 tablespoons lemon juice
- 2 garlic cloves, crushed
- 1 teaspoon peeled and grated fresh root ginger
- 1 teaspoon chilli powder
- 1 tablespoon clear honey
- 1 teaspoon sea salt

Mix together the marinade ingredients in a non-metallic bowl. Add the prawns and mix well. Leave to marinate for about 10 minutes.

Thread 2 prawns and 2 pieces of mango alternately on to each of 8 presoaked wooden skewers. Place the skewers on a foil-lined grill rack, brush with the remaining marinade and cook under a preheated hot grill for 2 minutes on each side or until the prawns turn pink and are cooked through.

Arrange some undressed salad on 4 serving plates and top each with 2 skewers. Serve hot.

TOP TIP

Try having an early night if you feel very hungry at the end of a fast day. Then you can go to sleep safe in the knowledge that you can have a hearty breakfast first thing in the morning.

Tiger prawns with pancetta

PREPARATION TIME **5 MINUTES** • COOKING TIME **7–8 MINUTES**

187 CALORIES PER SERVING

SERVES 2

- ½ teaspoon olive oil
- 7.5 g (¼ oz) unsalted butter
- 25 g (1 oz) pancetta or smoked bacon, finely chopped
- 250 g (8 oz) raw peeled tiger prawns
- grated rind and juice of ½ lemon
- 1 small bunch of watercress

Heat the oil and butter in a large frying pan, add the pancetta or smoked bacon and fry for 3–4 minutes until crisp.

Add the prawns and fry for 1 minute on each side or until they turn pink. Sprinkle over the lemon rind and juice and fry for a further 1 minute, then add the watercress and combine well. Serve hot.

Salt & pepper squid

272
CALORIES
PER SERVING

SERVES
4

- 500 g (1 lb) squid tubes, 10–12 cm (4–5 inches) long, cleaned
- ½ teaspoon Sichuan peppercorns, crushed
- ¼ teaspoon black peppercorns, crushed
- ½ teaspoon sea salt
- 4 tablespoons sunflower oil
- 1 medium-strength red chilli, deseeded and thinly sliced

Salad
- ½ cucumber, peeled
- 50 g (2 oz) watercress
- 2 spring onions, shredded
- 2 tablespoons dark soy sauce
- 2 tablespoons sesame oil
- 2 teaspoons caster sugar

To make the salad, cut the cucumber into long, fine strips and toss with the watercress and spring onions. Mix the soy sauce, sesame oil and sugar in a small bowl.

Halve each squid lengthways to form 2 flat triangles. Using the tip of a small, sharp knife, score the inner side of each piece making sure you don't cut right through. Pat the pieces dry on kitchen paper. Mix together the peppers and sea salt.

Heat 2 tablespoons of the oil in a large frying pan or wok, add the chilli and fry for 15–30 seconds until it begins to colour. Drain with a slotted spoon and set aside. Add half the squid and fry for 2–3 minutes or until it starts to colour. Drain with a slotted spoon and set aside. Repeat with the remaining oil and squid.

Return all the squid to the pan and sprinkle with the salt and pepper mixture, stir-frying until evenly coated. Transfer to 4 serving plates and scatter with the fried chilli. Divide the salad among the plates and drizzle with the dressing. Serve immediately.

Crab Malabar Hill

176 CALORIES PER SERVING

SERVES 2

1 tablespoon vegetable oil
1½ garlic cloves, finely chopped
1 teaspoon peeled and finely chopped fresh root ginger
3 spring onions, very thinly sliced
1½ red chillies, deseeded and finely sliced
300 g (10 oz) canned white crabmeat, drained
grated rind and juice of ½ lime
2 tablespoons chopped coriander
1 tablespoon chopped mint
salt and pepper
crisp lettuce leaves, to serve

Heat the oil in a large wok or frying pan until hot, then add the garlic, ginger, spring onions and chillies and stir-fry for 2–3 minutes.

Add the crabmeat, lime rind and juice, coriander and mint and stir-fry for a further 2–3 minutes, then season with salt and pepper. Serve hot on crisp lettuce leaves.

TOP TIP

Reward yourself for your successes. Set yourself targets and, once you have reached them, treat yourself to something nice.

Split pea & pepper patties

PREPARATION TIME **15 MINUTES, PLUS CHILLING** • COOKING TIME **45–50 MINUTES**

312 CALORIES PER SERVING

SERVES 4

750 ml (1¼ pints)
vegetable stock
3 garlic cloves
250 g (8 oz) yellow split
peas
olive oil spray
2 red peppers, halved,
cored and deseeded
1 yellow pepper, halved,
cored and deseeded
1 red onion, quartered
1 tablespoon chopped mint,
plus extra leaves to garnish
2 tablespoons capers,
drained and chopped
flour, for dusting
salt and pepper

Tzatziki
½ cucumber, finely
chopped
1 garlic clove, crushed
2 tablespoons chopped
mint
300 ml (½ pint) low fat
natural yogurt

Bring the stock to the boil in a large saucepan. Peel and halve 1 of the garlic cloves, then add to the pan with the split peas and cook for 40 minutes until the split peas are tender. Season with salt and pepper and leave to cool slightly.

Meanwhile, lightly spray a roasting tin with oil. Place the remaining garlic cloves in the tin with the peppers and onion and cook in a preheated oven, 200°C (400°F), Gas Mark 6, for 20 minutes. Squeeze the roasted garlic cloves from their skins and chop with the roasted vegetables.

Mix together the split peas, roasted vegetables, mint and capers in a large bowl. Flour your hands and shape the mixture into 12 patties. Chill until ready to cook.

To make the Tzatziki, mix the ingredients together, cover and chill in the refrigerator for about 30 minutes before serving.

Heat a frying pan and spray with oil. Cook the patties, in batches if necessary, for 2 minutes on each side. Serve 3 patties per person, hot or cold, garnished with mint leaves and with a small bowl of tzatziki.

Pea, egg & tofu curry

PREPARATION TIME **10 MINUTES** • COOKING TIME **15 MINUTES**

257 CALORIES PER SERVING

SERVES **4**

- 4 hard-boiled eggs
- ½ teaspoon ground turmeric
- 3 tablespoons vegetable oil
- 1 bay leaf
- 2 onions, finely chopped
- 2 garlic cloves, finely chopped
- 1½ teaspoons ground coriander
- 1½ teaspoons ground garam masala
- ½ teaspoon chilli powder
- 1 tablespoon tomato purée
- 125 g (4 oz) canned tomatoes, chopped
- 125 ml (4 fl oz) water
- 125 g (4 oz) tofu, cut into 1 cm (½ inch) cubes
- 1 tablespoon natural yogurt
- 100 g (3½ oz) frozen peas
- 2 tablespoons finely chopped coriander
- salt and pepper

Shell the eggs and coat well in the turmeric. Heat the oil in a large frying pan and lightly fry the eggs over a medium heat for 2 minutes, then remove from the pan and set aside.

Add the bay leaf, onions and garlic to the pan and cook over a medium heat for 2 minutes. Stir in the spices and cook for a further 1 minute. Add the tomato purée, tomatoes and measurement water, cover and cook for 5 minutes.

Return the eggs to the pan with the tofu, yogurt and peas. Season with a little salt and pepper.

Cook for 5 minutes, then remove the bay leaf, sprinkle with the chopped coriander and serve.

Spicy aubergine curry

PREPARATION TIME **15 MINUTES** • COOKING TIME **20 MINUTES**

231
CALORIES
PER SERVING

SERVES
4

- 1 teaspoon cumin seeds
- 4 teaspoons coriander seeds
- 1 teaspoon cayenne pepper
- 2 green chillies, deseeded and sliced
- ½ teaspoon ground turmeric
- 4 garlic cloves, crushed
- 2.5 cm (1 inch) piece of fresh root ginger, peeled and grated
- 300 ml (½ pint) warm water
- 400 g (13 oz) can reduced fat coconut milk
- 1 tablespoon tamarind paste
- 1 large aubergine, thinly sliced lengthways
- salt and pepper
- 4 mini plain naan breads, to serve

Dry-fry the cumin and coriander seeds in a small, nonstick frying pan for a few minutes until aromatic and toasted. Leave to cool, then crush together.

Mix together the crushed seeds, cayenne, chillies, turmeric, garlic, ginger and the measurement water in a large saucepan and simmer for 10 minutes until thickened. Season with salt and pepper, then stir in the coconut milk and tamarind paste.

Arrange the aubergine slices on a foil-lined grill rack and brush the tops with some of the curry sauce. Cook under a preheated hot grill until golden.

Stir the aubergine slices into the curry sauce. Serve hot with naan bread.

Squash with red bean sauce

PREPARATION TIME **15 MINUTES** • COOKING TIME **18 MINUTES**

247 CALORIES PER SERVING

SERVES 4

- 600 ml (1 pint) vegetable stock
- 1 kg (2 lb) mixed baby squash, such as gem, butternut or acorn, peeled, quartered and deseeded
- 125 g (4 oz) baby spinach leaves

Bean sauce
- 4 tablespoons olive oil
- 4 garlic cloves, thinly sliced
- 1 red pepper, cored, deseeded and finely chopped
- 2 tomatoes, chopped
- 425 g (14 oz) can red kidney beans, rinsed and drained
- 1–2 tablespoons hot chilli sauce
- small handful of chopped coriander
- salt

Bring the stock to the boil in a large saucepan, then add the squash. Reduce the heat, cover and simmer gently for about 15 minutes or until just tender.

Meanwhile, make the sauce. Heat the oil in a frying pan, add the garlic and red pepper and fry for 5 minutes, stirring frequently, until very soft. Add the tomatoes, kidney beans, chilli sauce and a little salt and simmer for 5 minutes until pulpy.

Drain the squash, reserving the stock, and return to the saucepan. Scatter over the spinach leaves, cover and cook for about 1 minute until the spinach has wilted.

Pile the vegetables on to 4 serving plates. Stir 8 tablespoons of the reserved stock into the sauce and add the coriander. Spoon the sauce over the vegetables and serve.

Chicken with celeriac cakes

PREPARATION TIME **15 MINUTES** • COOKING TIME **20 MINUTES**

312 CALORIES PER SERVING

SERVES **4**

- 1 large head of celeriac, about 400 g (13 oz), peeled
- 1 garlic clove, finely chopped
- 1 small onion, finely chopped
- 2 back bacon rashers, cut into short strips
- 2 dessertspoons walnuts, crushed
- 25 g (1 oz) Cheddar cheese, grated
- 1 egg white
- 1 tablespoon olive oil
- 4 corn-fed chicken breast fillets, about 150 g (5 oz) each, with skin on
- salt and pepper

Sauce
- 300 ml (½ pint) apple juice
- 150 ml (¼ pint) chicken stock
- 1 cooking apple, peeled and grated

Cut 4 thin, round slices from the celeriac and set aside. Grate the remaining celeriac and combine with the garlic, onion, bacon and walnuts in a nonstick frying pan. Cover and sweat for 4 minutes or until soft.

Remove the pan from the heat, add the cheese and egg white and stir to mix thoroughly. Season with salt and pepper. Divide the mixture into 4 portions and, when cool enough to handle, shape into 4 cakes.

Place the cakes on a nonstick baking sheet and bake in a preheated oven, 220°C (425°F), Gas Mark 7, for 15 minutes or until golden.

Meanwhile, brush the reserved celeriac slices with the oil and place on a grill rack. Season the chicken breasts and place each one, skin side down, on a celeriac slice. Cook under a preheated medium grill for 4 minutes, then turn the chicken over and cook for a further 5–6 minutes or until cooked through.

To make the sauce, pour the apple juice and stock into a saucepan and boil rapidly until reduced by two-thirds. Add the grated apple and remove the pan from the heat.

Transfer the celeriac cakes on to 4 serving plates and top with the chicken breasts. Use kitchen paper to remove any excess fat from the celeriac slices. Pour a little sauce around the chicken and garnish with the celeriac slices. Serve immediately.

Blackened chicken skewers

PREPARATION TIME **10 MINUTES, PLUS MARINATING** • COOKING TIME **20 MINUTES**

94 CALORIES PER SERVING

SERVES 2

- 150 g (5 oz) boneless, skinless chicken breast, diced
- ½ tablespoon Cajun seasoning mix
- 1 tablespoon lemon juice
- ½ teaspoon olive oil
- coriander sprigs, to garnish

Put the chicken in a bowl and add the seasoning mix, lemon juice and oil. Toss well and leave to marinate for 15 minutes.

Thread the chicken on to 4 presoaked wooden skewers and cover the ends of the skewers with foil. Cook under a preheated medium grill for 20 minutes or until cooked through, turning halfway through cooking. Remove the skewers from the grill and reserve any juices.

Slide the chicken from the skewers on to 2 serving plates, allowing 2 skewers per person, and garnish with sprigs of coriander. Serve immediately with the juices poured over.

TOP TIP

If hunger is getting the better of you, try taking a brisk walk round the block or running up and down the stairs five times – anything to take your mind of that grumbling tummy.

Lemon & rosemary chicken

PREPARATION TIME **5 MINUTES** • COOKING TIME **25–30 MINUTES**

363 CALORIES PER SERVING

SERVES 4

- 4 chicken breast fillets, about 150 g (5 oz) each, with skin on
- 2 tablespoons olive oil
- 15 g (½ oz) butter
- 1 rosemary sprig or 1 teaspoon dried rosemary
- 3 garlic cloves, roughly sliced
- 250 ml (8 fl oz) dry white wine
- 2 tablespoons lemon juice
- 5–6 very thin strips of lemon rind
- salt and pepper

Rinse the chicken under cold running water and place skin side down in a sauté pan. Dry-fry the chicken over a medium heat until it is evenly browned on all sides.

Add the oil, butter, rosemary, garlic and salt and pepper, then cook for 2–3 minutes, turning the chicken pieces once. Add the wine, increase the heat and let the wine bubble for about 1 minute.

Reduce the heat to medium-low, cover and cook for 15–20 minutes or until the chicken is cooked through and still juicy.

Remove the pan from the heat and transfer the chicken to a warm serving dish. Skim the oil off the surface of the liquid, then add the lemon juice and rind and cook over a medium heat for 1 minute, stirring gently. Pour the sauce over the chicken and serve.

Carnival chicken

PREPARATION TIME **15 MINUTES, PLUS MARINATING** • COOKING TIME **20 MINUTES**

300 CALORIES PER SERVING

SERVES 4

- **4 skinless chicken breasts, about 140 g (5 oz) each**
- **flat leaf parsley sprigs, to garnish**

Marinade
- **100 ml (3½ fl oz) sweet sherry**
- **1 teaspoon Angostura bitters**
- **1 tablespoon light soy sauce**
- **1 tablespoon peeled and chopped fresh root ginger**
- **pinch of ground cumin**
- **pinch of ground coriander**
- **1 teaspoon dried mixed herbs**
- **1 small onion, finely chopped**
- **75 ml (3 fl oz) chicken stock**

Sweet potato mash
- **500 g (1 lb) sweet potatoes**
- **salt and pepper**

Place the chicken breasts in a non-metallic dish. Mix together the marinade ingredients in a bowl, then spoon over the chicken, making sure the pieces are well coated. Cover and leave to marinate in the refrigerator overnight.

Cook the chicken under a preheated medium grill for 20 minutes or until cooked through, turning halfway through cooking. Remove from the grill and keep warm.

Meanwhile, boil the sweet potatoes in their skins for 20 minutes until soft. Drain well, then peel. Mash the potato and leave it to dry off slightly. Season with salt and pepper and serve with the chicken, garnished with sprigs of parsley.

Chicken & spinach curry

PREPARATION TIME **10 MINUTES** • COOKING TIME **25 MINUTES**

205 CALORIES PER SERVING

SERVES 4

1 tablespoon vegetable oil
4 boneless, skinless
chicken breasts, about
125 g (4 oz) each, halved
lengthways
1 onion, sliced
2 garlic cloves, chopped
1 green chilli, chopped
4 cardamom pods, lightly
crushed
1 teaspoon cumin seeds
1 teaspoon dried chilli
flakes
1 teaspoon ground ginger
1 teaspoon ground
turmeric
250 g (8 oz) baby spinach
leaves
300 g (10 oz) tomatoes,
chopped
150 ml (¼ pint) low-fat
Greek yogurt
2 tablespoons chopped
coriander, plus extra
sprigs to garnish
boiled rice, to serve
(optional)

Heat the oil in a large frying pan or wok, add the chicken, onion, garlic and chilli and fry for 4–5 minutes or until the chicken begins to brown and the onion to soften. Add the cardamoms, cumin seeds, chilli flakes, ginger and turmeric and fry for a further 1 minute.

Add the spinach, cover and cook gently until the spinach wilts, then stir in the tomatoes, re-cover and simmer for 15 minutes or until the chicken is cooked through, removing the lid for the last 5 minutes of cooking.

Stir the yogurt and coriander into the curry and garnished with sprigs of coriander. Serve with boiled rice, if liked (remembering to count the calories).

Lime & chilli chicken kebabs

PREPARATION TIME **15–20 MINUTES, PLUS MARINATING** • COOKING TIME **10 MINUTES**

381 CALORIES PER SERVING

SERVES **2**

- about 250 g (8 oz) boneless, skinless chicken breast, cut into strips
- 1 lime, halved
- 100 g (3½ oz) rice noodles
- salt and pepper
- 1 tablespoon chopped coriander, to garnish

Marinade
- grated rind and juice of 1 lime
- 1 garlic clove, chopped
- 1 tablespoon chopped dried or fresh red chilli
- 25 ml (1 fl oz) sunflower oil

Mix together the marinade ingredients in a non-metallic bowl. Add the chicken, mix well and season with salt and pepper. Cover and leave to marinate in the refrigerator for 1 hour.

Thread the chicken evenly on to 6 presoaked wooden skewers. Cook the kebabs and lime halves under a preheated hot grill or in a preheated griddle pan for about 10 minutes or until the chicken is cooked through.

Meanwhile, bring a large saucepan of water to the boil, then turn off the heat and add the rice noodles. Cover and leave to cook for 3–4 minutes, or according to the packet instructions, until just tender, then drain.

Garnish the chicken with the coriander and serve 3 skewers per person with the noodles and caramelized lime halves.

Tandoori chicken

PREPARATION TIME **10 MINUTES, PLUS MARINATING** • COOKING TIME **20 MINUTES**

175 CALORIES PER SERVING

SERVES 4

4 chicken breast fillets, about 140 g (4½ oz) each
wine or water
a few herb sprigs, such as rosemary, thyme or parsley

Marinade
1 tablespoon peeled and grated fresh root ginger
2 teaspoons coriander seeds, toasted
2 teaspoons rosemary leaves
1 teaspoon grated lemon rind
½ teaspoon ground cardamom
½ teaspoon ground cumin
¼ teaspoon crushed black peppercorns
¼ teaspoon chilli sauce or powder
125 g (4 oz) natural yogurt
1 tablespoon lemon juice

Mix together the marinade ingredients in a bowl. Place the chicken in a non-metallic dish. Spoon over the marinade and rub well into the chicken. Cover and leave to marinate in the refrigerator for 2–4 hours.

Scrape the excess marinade from the chicken and discard. Place the chicken on a wire rack set in a roasting tin. Pour in wine or water to the depth of 2.5 cm (1 inch) and add the herb sprigs, to keep the meat moist during cooking.

Bake the chicken in a preheated oven, 240°C (475°F), Gas Mark 9, for 10 minutes. Turn the chicken over, return to the oven and bake for a further 10 minutes or until cooked through.

Cranberry chicken stir-fry

PREPARATION TIME **15 MINUTES** • COOKING TIME **10 MINUTES**

230 CALORIES PER SERVING

SERVES **4**

- 2 tablespoons vegetable oil
- 2 shallots, finely chopped
- 2.5 cm (1 inch) piece of fresh root ginger, peeled and thinly sliced into matchsticks
- 2 garlic cloves, crushed
- 300 g (10 oz) boneless, skinless chicken breast, thinly sliced
- 2 tablespoons hoisin sauce
- 2 tablespoons oyster sauce
- 1 tablespoon light soy sauce
- 150 g (5 oz) dried cranberries
- 4 spring onions, diagonally sliced
- 125 g (4 oz) bean sprouts, sliced

Basil and chilli garnish
- vegetable oil, for deep-frying
- handful of basil leaves
- 1 large red chilli, deseeded and thinly sliced

Heat the 2 tablespoons oil in a wok, add the shallots, ginger and garlic and stir-fry over a medium heat for 30 seconds. Add the chicken and stir-fry for 2 minutes or until golden brown.

Add the hoisin, oyster and soy sauces and the cranberries and stir-fry for a further 2 minutes until the chicken is cooked through, then add the spring onions and bean sprouts and toss together for 3–4 minutes.

To make the garnish, heat 1 cm (½ inch) of oil in a small saucepan, then deep-fry the basil leaves and red chilli, in 2 batches, for 10–30 seconds until crisp. Remove with a slotted spoon and drain on kitchen paper.

Serve the stir-fry garnished with the deep-fried basil and chilli.

Chicken with spring vegetables

PREPARATION TIME **10 MINUTES, PLUS RESTING** • COOKING TIME **ABOUT 1¼ HOURS**

370 CALORIES PER SERVING

SERVES 4

1.5 kg (3 lb) chicken
about 1.5 litres (2½ pints) hot chicken stock
2 shallots, halved
2 garlic cloves
2 parsley sprigs
2 marjoram sprigs
2 lemon thyme sprigs
2 carrots, halved
1 leek, trimmed and sliced
200 g (7 oz) Tenderstem broccoli
250 g (8 oz) asparagus, trimmed
½ Savoy cabbage, shredded

Put the chicken in a large saucepan and pour over enough stock to just cover the chicken. Push the shallots, garlic, herbs, carrots and leek into the pan and bring to the boil over a medium-high heat, then reduce the heat and simmer gently for 1 hour or until the chicken is falling away from the bones.

Add the remaining vegetables to the pan and simmer for a further 6–8 minutes or until the vegetables are cooked.

Turn off the heat and leave to rest for 5–10 minutes. Remove the skin from the chicken, if liked, then divide the chicken among 4 deep serving bowls with the vegetables. Serve with spoonfuls of the broth ladled over.

Asian steamed chicken salad

PREPARATION TIME **10 MINUTES, PLUS COOLING** • COOKING TIME **8–10 MINUTES**

273 CALORIES PER SERVING SERVES **2**

- 2 chicken breasts fillets, about 150 g (5 oz) each
- ¼ small Chinese cabbage, finely shredded
- ½ large carrot, grated
- 125 g (4 oz) bean sprouts
- handful of coriander, finely chopped
- handful of mint, finely chopped
- ½ red chilli, deseeded and finely sliced (optional)

Dressing
- 40 ml (1½ fl oz) sunflower oil
- juice of 1 lime
- ¾ tablespoon Thai fish sauce
- 1½ tablespoons light soy sauce
- ½ tablespoon peeled and finely chopped fresh root ginger

Put the chicken in a bamboo or other steamer set over a large saucepan of boiling water, cover and cook for about 8 minutes or until the chicken is cooked through. Alternatively, poach the chicken for 8–10 minutes until cooked and tender.

Meanwhile, make the dressing by combining all the ingredient in a screw-top jar.

When the chicken is cool enough to handle, cut or tear it into strips and mix the pieces with 1 tablespoon of the dressing in a bowl. Leave to cool.

Toss together all the vegetables, herbs and chilli, if using, in a large bowl, then divide among 2 serving bowls. Scatter over the cold chicken and serve immediately with the remaining salad dressing.

Tea-infused duck with pak choi

PREPARATION TIME **20 MINUTES, PLUS INFUSING** • COOKING TIME **10 MINUTES**

148 CALORIES PER SERVING

SERVES 6

3 teaspoons green tea or
3 teabags
250 ml (8 fl oz) boiling
water
3 duck breasts, about 150 g
(5 oz) each, with skin on
3 tablespoons soy sauce
250 g (8 oz) carrots, cut
into matchsticks
4 small pak choi, about
400 g (13 oz) in total,
leaves and stems thickly
sliced but kept separate
3 spring onions, sliced
2 tablespoons orange
liqueur
juice of 1 orange

Make the tea using the boiling water, leave to infuse for 5 minutes, then strain and cool.

Make crisscross cuts in the duck skin and place the duck, skin side up, in a shallow glass or china dish. Pour the tea over the duck breasts, cover and leave to infuse in the refrigerator for 3–4 hours or overnight.

Place the duck breasts in a roasting tin, drizzle 1 tablespoon of the soy sauce over the skin and roast in a preheated oven, 220°C (425°F), Gas Mark 7, for 10 minutes until the skin is crispy but the meat is still slightly pink. After 5 minutes, transfer 2 teaspoons of fat from the tin to a frying pan or wok.

Reheat the fat, add the carrots and stir-fry for 2 minutes. Add the pak choi stems and cook for 1 minute. Add the pak choi leaves, spring onions and the remaining soy sauce and cook for 30 seconds. Pour on the liqueur, light with a match and stand well back. When the flames subside, pour in the orange juice and warm through.

Spoon the vegetables into 6 small dishes and top with drained and thinly sliced duck breast. Serve immediately.

Turkey ragout

PREPARATION TIME **10 MINUTES** • COOKING TIME **1 HOUR 50 MINUTES**

190 CALORIES PER SERVING

SERVES **4**

- 1 turkey drumstick, about 625 g (1¼ lb)
- 2 garlic cloves
- 15 baby onions or shallots
- 3 carrots, diagonally sliced
- 300 ml (½ pint) red wine
- a few thyme sprigs
- 2 bay leaves
- 2 tablespoons chopped flat leaf parsley
- 1 teaspoon port wine jelly
- 1 teaspoon wholegrain mustard
- salt and pepper

Carefully remove the skin from the turkey drumstick and make a few cuts in the flesh. Finely slice 1 of the garlic cloves and push the slivers into the slashes. Crush the remaining garlic clove.

Transfer the drumstick to a large, flameproof casserole or roasting tin with the onions or shallots, carrots, crushed garlic, red wine, thyme and bay leaves. Season well with salt and pepper, cover and place in a preheated oven, 180°C (350°F), Gas Mark 4, for about 1¾ hours or until the turkey is cooked through.

Remove the turkey and vegetables from the casserole and keep hot. Bring the sauce to the boil on the hob, discarding the bay leaves. Add the parsley, port wine jelly and mustard. Boil for 5 minutes, until slightly thickened. Season with salt and pepper. Carve the turkey and serve with the juices in 4 serving bowls.

Plaice with coconut crust

PREPARATION TIME **10 MINUTES** • COOKING TIME **15 MINUTES**

195
CALORIES
PER SERVING

SERVES
2

- 15 g (½ oz) desiccated coconut
- 25 g (1 oz) fresh breadcrumbs
- 1 tablespoon chopped chives
- small pinch of paprika
- 2 skinless plaice fillets, about 125 g (4 oz) each
- salt and pepper
- lime wedges, to serve

Mix together the coconut, breadcrumbs, chives and paprika in a bowl and season with salt and pepper.

Arrange the fish fillets on a baking sheet and top each one with the coconut mixture.

Place in a preheated oven, 180°C (350°F), Gas Mark 4, for 15 minutes or until cooked through. Serve with lime wedges.

Griddled tuna with shallot jus

PREPARATION TIME **5 MINUTES** • COOKING TIME **15 MINUTES**

240
CALORIES
PER SERVING

SERVES
2

- 2 tuna steaks, about 100 g (3½ oz) each
- flat leaf parsley sprigs, to garnish

Shallot jus
- 2 shallots, finely chopped
- 150 ml (¼ pint) red wine
- 75 ml (⅛ pint) Marsala
- salt and pepper

Heat a griddle or frying pan until it is very hot, add the tuna steaks and cook for 3 minutes on each side. Remove from the pan and keep warm.

To make the shallot jus, mix all the ingredients in a saucepan, season with salt and pepper and boil rapidly until the sauce is reduced by half. Return the tuna steaks to the frying pan, add the sauce and simmer for 2 minutes. Serve immediately, garnished with parsley sprigs.

Masala roast cod

150 CALORIES PER SERVING

SERVES 4

- 1 red chilli, chopped
- 2 garlic cloves, chopped
- 1 teaspoon peeled and minced fresh root ginger
- 1 teaspoon mustard seeds
- large pinch of ground turmeric
- 2 cloves
- 2 cardamom pods
- 5 peppercorns
- 3 tablespoons water
- 1 teaspoon olive oil
- 3 tablespoons low-fat natural yogurt
- 25 g (1 oz) fresh breadcrumbs
- 500 g (1 lb) cod fillet
- 250 g (8 oz) ripe tomatoes, chopped

To serve
- coriander leaves
- strips of lemon rind
- lemon and lime wedges

Place the chilli, garlic, ginger, mustard seeds, turmeric, cloves, cardamoms, peppercorns and measurement water in a blender or coffee grinder and blend to form a paste. Alternatively, use a pestle and mortar.

Heat the oil in a small saucepan and fry the chilli paste until the oil comes to the surface. Remove the pan from the heat and stir in the yogurt and breadcrumbs.

Place the cod in an ovenproof dish and spread the chilli paste over it. Scatter over the tomatoes, cover with foil and place in a preheated oven, 200°C (400°F), Gas Mark 6, for 30 minutes or until the fish is cooked through and tender.

Divide the cod among 4 serving plates, sprinkle with coriander leaves and strips of lemon rind and serve with lemon and lime wedges.

Red mullet with baked tomatoes

PREPARATION TIME **20 MINUTES** • COOKING TIME **18–20 MINUTES**

287 CALORIES PER SERVING

SERVES 4

- 8 red mullet fillets, about 100 g (3½ oz) each, scaled and gutted
- finely grated rind of 1 lemon
- 2 teaspoons baby capers, drained
- 2 spring onions, finely sliced
- 375 g (12 oz) mixed red and yellow cherry tomatoes
- 150 g (5 oz) fine green beans, trimmed
- 2 garlic cloves, finely chopped
- 50 g (2 oz) can anchovies, drained and chopped
- 1 tablespoon olive oil
- 2 tablespoons lemon juice
- salt and pepper

To garnish
- 2 tablespoons chopped parsley
- 8 caperberries

Tear off 4 large sheets of foil and line with nonstick baking paper. Place 2 fish fillets on each piece of baking paper, then scatter over the lemon rind, capers and spring onions and season with salt and pepper. Fold over the paper-lined foil and scrunch the edges together to seal. Place the parcels on a large baking sheet.

Put the cherry tomatoes in an ovenproof dish with the green beans, garlic, anchovies, oil and lemon juice. Season with salt and pepper and mix well.

Bake the vegetables in a preheated oven, 200°C (400°F), Gas Mark 6, for 10 minutes until tender. Place the fish next to the vegetables in the oven and bake for a further 8–10 minutes until the flesh flakes easily when pressed in the centre with a knife.

Spoon the vegetables on to 4 serving plates, then top each with 2 steamed fish fillets. Sprinkle over the chopped parsley, garnish with the caperberries and serve immediately.

Halibut with papaya salsa

PREPARATION TIME **15 MINUTES** • COOKING TIME **10–12 MINUTES**

236 CALORIES PER SERVING

SERVES **4**

- 2 teaspoons olive oil
- 3 garlic cloves, crushed
- 4 halibut steaks, about 600 g (1¼ lb) in total

Salsa
- 1 papaya, cut into cubes
- ½ red onion, finely chopped
- 15 g (½ oz) coriander leaves, finely chopped
- ¼–½ teaspoon red chilli powder
- 1 red pepper, cored, deseeded and finely chopped
- juice of ½ lime

To serve
- watercress leaves
- lime wedges

Heat the oil in a large frying pan, add the garlic and stir for a few seconds. Add the fish and fry for 10–12 minutes until just cooked through, turning halfway through cooking.

Meanwhile, make the salsa by mixing together all the ingredients in a bowl.

Serve the halibut steaks on a bed of watercress leaves, with the salsa and lime wedges.

Aromatic tamarind fish broth

PREPARATION TIME **10 MINUTES** • COOKING TIME **12–15 MINUTES**

123 CALORIES PER SERVING

SERVES 4

50 g (2 oz) coriander, with roots attached
4 cm (1½ inch) cube of peeled fresh root ginger
25 g (1 oz) onion, roughly chopped
1 teaspoon shrimp or anchovy paste, or
1 anchovy fillet
3 tablespoons water
750 ml (1¼ pints) hot chicken stock
1 tablespoon tamarind paste or 2 teaspoons lime juice
1 teaspoon dark brown sugar
¼ teaspoon salt
500 g (1 lb) thick white fish fillets, such as cod, haddock or halibut, cut into 10 cm (4 inch) cubes
1 spring onion, finely sliced

Cut the roots off the coriander and roughly chop, then chop the rest of the herb and reserve.

Roughly chop three-quarters of the ginger and cut the remainder into matchsticks.

Place the coriander roots, chopped ginger, onion, fish paste or anchovy fillet and measurement water in a blender or food processor and blend to a purée.

Pour the stock into a frying pan and add the purée, tamarind paste or lime juice, sugar and salt and bring to a simmer, then simmer for 5 minutes. Season to taste, if necessary.

Put the fish in the pan and poach for 1 minute. Gently turn the fish over and cook for a further 5–8 minutes, basting frequently, until cooked through.

Transfer the fish to a large serving dish. Pour over the poaching liquid, scatter with the spring onion, the ginger strips and the reserved coriander and serve.

Grilled sardines with tabbouleh

PREPARATION TIME **15 MINUTES** • COOKING TIME **15 MINUTES**

209 CALORIES PER SERVING

SERVES **4**

- **125 g (4 oz) bulgar wheat**
- **1 onion, finely chopped**
- **2 ripe tomatoes**
- **1 tablespoon lemon juice**
- **1 teaspoon grated lemon rind**
- **small handful of mint leaves**
- **4 small sardines, gutted and boned**
- **salt and pepper**

To serve
- **lemon wedges**
- **salad or herb leaves**

Cook the bulgar wheat in a small saucepan of boiling water for 5 minutes, then drain and refresh under cold running water. Drain again and put into a bowl.

Meanwhile, dry-fry the onion in a small, nonstick frying pan for 5 minutes. Put the tomatoes in a large saucepan or heatproof bowl and pour over enough boiling water to cover, then leave for about 1 minute. Drain, skin the tomatoes carefully, then deseed and finely chop the flesh.

Add the onion, tomatoes, lemon juice and rind to the bulgar wheat. Reserve 4 mint leaves, then chop the remainder. Stir the chopped mint into the bulgar wheat mixture and season with salt and pepper.

Open out each sardine and lay a mint leaf along the centre. Spoon over a little of the tabbouleh and carefully fold the fillet back over. Cook the sardines under a preheated grill for 5 minutes, then carefully turn them over and cook for a further 5 minutes or until cooked through. Serve with the remaining tabbouleh (hot or cold), lemon wedges and a few salad or herb leaves.

Sesame-crusted salmon

PREPARATION TIME **10 MINUTES** • COOKING TIME **9–12 MINUTES**

324 CALORIES PER SERVING

SERVES 2

2 tablespoons sesame
seeds
½ teaspoon dried chilli
flakes
2 salmon fillets, about
100 g (3½ oz) each
1 teaspoon olive oil
1 carrot, cut into
matchsticks
1 red pepper, cored,
deseeded and thinly sliced
100 g (3½ oz) shiitake
mushrooms, halved
1 pak choi, quartered
lengthways
2 spring onions, shredded
½ tablespoon soy sauce

Mix together the sesame seeds and chilli flakes on a plate, then
press the salmon fillets into the mixture until covered.

Heat half the oil in a frying pan or wok, add the salmon and
cook over a medium heat for 3–4 minutes on each side until
cooked through. Remove from the pan and keep warm.

Heat the remaining oil in the pan, add the vegetables and stir-
fry for 3–4 minutes until just cooked. Drizzle the soy sauce over
the vegetables, then serve with the salmon.

Chilli & coriander fish parcel

PREPARATION TIME **15 MINUTES, PLUS MARINATING AND CHILLING** • COOKING TIME **15 MINUTES**

127 CALORIES PER SERVING

SERVES 1

- 125 g (4 oz) cod, coley or haddock fillet
- 2 teaspoons lemon juice
- 1 tablespoon coriander leaves, plus extra to garnish
- 1 garlic clove
- 1 green chilli, deseeded and chopped, plus extra to garnish
- ¼ teaspoon sugar
- 2 teaspoons natural yogurt

Place the fish in a non-metallic dish and sprinkle with the lemon juice. Cover and leave to marinate in the refrigerator for 15–20 minutes.

Place the coriander, garlic and chilli in a mini food processor and blend until the mixture forms a paste. Add the sugar and yogurt and briefly process to blend.

Lay the fish on a sheet of baking parchment or foil and coat on both sides with the paste. Gather up the parchment or foil loosely around the fish and turn over at the top to seal. Chill for at least 1 hour.

Place the parcel on a baking sheet and bake in a preheated oven, 200°C (400°F), Gas Mark 6, for about 15 minutes or until the fish is just cooked through. Serve garnished with extra chilli and coriander.

Fish & tomato curry

PREPARATION TIME **10 MINUTES** • COOKING TIME **12–15 MINUTES**

194
CALORIES
PER SERVING

**SERVES
4**

2 tablespoons vegetable oil
1 onion, finely chopped
4 garlic cloves, sliced
1 teaspoon peeled and
grated fresh root ginger
½ teaspoon ground
turmeric
1 teaspoon chilli powder
1 teaspoon ground cumin
2 teaspoons ground
coriander
1 teaspoon garam masala
500 g (1 lb) thick white
fish fillets, such as cod or
haddock, cut into 2.5 cm
(1 inch) cubes
400 g (13 oz) can chopped
tomatoes
2 teaspoons sea salt
2 teaspoons sugar

Heat the oil in a large frying pan, add the onion and fry until soft and lightly browned. Add the garlic, ginger and spices and fry for 30 seconds. Add the fish and stir gently for a further 1 minute.

Add the tomatoes, salt and sugar and stir gently. Cover and simmer gently for 7–10 minutes or until the fish is cooked through. Serve hot.

TOP TIP

It takes 20 minutes for your brain to register that your stomach is full, so eating slowly is a great trick to stop you from overeating on your 'off' days.

Squid, chickpea & pepper stew

PREPARATION TIME **10 MINUTES** • COOKING TIME **25 MINUTES**

331 CALORIES PER SERVING

SERVES **1**

- 1 tablespoon plain flour
- 400 g (13 oz) ready-prepared squid rings
- 2 tablespoons olive oil
- 1 fennel bulb, trimmed and chopped
- 2 green peppers, cored, deseeded and sliced
- 2 garlic cloves, crushed
- 1 tablespoon chopped oregano
- 600 ml (1 pint) fish stock
- 400 g (13 oz) can chickpeas, rinsed and drained
- squeeze of lemon juice
- 8 cherry tomatoes, halved
- salt and pepper

Season the flour and use it to dust the squid rings. Heat the oil in a large saucepan, add the fennel and peppers and fry gently for 5 minutes. Add the garlic and oregano and fry for a further 5 minutes.

Add the squid and continue to fry for 5 minutes or until puffed into rings. Stir in the stock and chickpeas and bring to a simmer. Cook gently, covered, for 10 minutes.

Add the lemon juice and tomatoes and season with salt and pepper. Cook for a further 1 minute, then serve.

Lemony scallop skewers

PREPARATION TIME **10 MINUTES** • COOKING TIME **2–3 MINUTES**

238
CALORIES
PER SERVING

SERVES
2

200 g (6 oz) queen
scallops, without roes
finely grated rind of
½ lemon
1½ teaspoons basil oil
25 g (1 oz) blanched
hazelnuts
100 g (3½ oz) rocket
½ tablespoon lemon juice
salt and pepper

Put the scallops in a bowl with the lemon rind and 1 teaspoon of the basil oil and season with black pepper. Mix well to coat.

Thread the scallops on to 2 metal skewers and cook under a preheated grill for 2–3 minutes, turning occasionally, until just cooked through, firm and opaque.

Meanwhile, heat a small frying pan over a medium heat, then tip in the hazelnuts and dry-fry until golden, shaking the pan frequently. Tip the nuts into a small dish and crush lightly.

Toss the rocket with the remaining basil oil, the lemon juice and salt and pepper. Arrange on 2 serving plates and top each with a scallop skewer. Scatter over the hazelnuts and serve immediately.

Aromatic steamed mussels

PREPARATION TIME **20 MINUTES** • COOKING TIME **15–17 MINUTES**

185 CALORIES PER SERVING

SERVES **2**

- 750 g (1½ lb) fresh mussels, soaked in cold water
- ½ tablespoon groundnut oil
- 1 shallot, thinly sliced
- ½ red chilli, deseeded and finely sliced
- 1.25 cm (½ inch) piece of fresh root ginger, peeled and finely chopped
- ½ garlic clove, finely sliced
- 1½ tablespoons anise-flavoured liqueur, such as Pernod
- 175 ml (6 fl oz) fish or vegetable stock
- ½ small preserved lemon, finely chopped
- ½ small bunch of coriander, roughly chopped
- salt and pepper

Discard any mussels that are open or have cracked shells. Scrub with a small nailbrush, remove any barnacles and pull off any small, hairy beards. Return the mussels to a bowl of clean cold water.

Heat the oil in a large, heavy-based casserole over a medium-low heat, then stir in the shallot, chilli, ginger and garlic and cook gently for 7–8 minutes or until softened, stirring occasionally. Add the alcohol and simmer until evaporated, then add the stock and preserved lemon and bring to the boil.

Drain the mussels and tip into the pan. Season with salt and pepper, then stir the mussels to coat them in the shallot mixture. Cover with a tight-fitting lid and steam gently, shaking the pan occasionally, for 4–5 minutes. Halfway through cooking use a large metal spoon to stir the mussels thoroughly, lifting the ones from the bottom of the pan to the top. Replace the lid and cook until the mussels have opened.

Heap the mussels into 2 deep serving bowls, discarding any shells that have not opened. Scatter over the coriander and serve immediately with a large bowl to the side for the empty shells.

Clams with chorizo & pimentón

PREPARATION TIME **25 MINUTES** • COOKING TIME **15–17 MINUTES**

257
CALORIES
PER SERVING

SERVES
4

1.5 kg (3 lb) fresh clams, soaked in cold water
750 g (1½ lb) tomatoes
2 tablespoons olive oil
1 large onion, finely chopped
2–3 garlic cloves, finely chopped
¼ teaspoon ground pimentón (smoked paprika)
400 ml (14 fl oz) fish stock
75 g (3 oz) sliced chorizo sausage, diced
salt and pepper
chopped parsley, to garnish

Discard any clams that are open or have cracked shells. Scrub with a small nailbrush, remove any barnacles and pull off any small, hairy beards. Return the clams to a bowl of clean cold water.

Put the tomatoes in a large saucepan or heatproof bowl and pour over enough boiling water to cover, then leave for about 1 minute. Drain, skin the tomatoes carefully and then deseed and dice the flesh.

Heat the oil in a large saucepan, add the onion and fry for 5 minutes until softened and lightly browned. Stir in the garlic and pimentón and cook for a further 1 minute. Stir in the tomatoes, stock and chorizo, season with salt and pepper and simmer for 3–4 minutes.

Drain the clams and tip them into the pan, cover with a tight-fitting lid and cook for 5–7 minutes until the clams have opened. Spoon the clams and the sauce into 4 shallow serving bowls, discarding any shells that have not opened. Garnish with parsley and serve immediately.

Seafood zarzuela

240 CALORIES PER SERVING

SERVES 4

- 500 g (1 lb) tomatoes
- 1 tablespoon olive oil
- 1 large onion, finely chopped
- 2 garlic cloves, finely chopped
- ½ teaspoon pimentón (smoked paprika)
- 1 red pepper, cored, deseeded and diced
- 200 ml (7 fl oz) fish stock
- 150 ml (¼ pint) dry white wine
- 2 large pinches of saffron threads
- 4 small bay leaves
- 500 g (1 lb) fresh mussels, soaked in cold water
- 200 g (7 oz) squid, cleaned and rinsed in cold water
- 375 g (12 oz) skinless cod loin, cubed
- salt and pepper

Put the tomatoes in a large saucepan or heatproof bowl and pour over enough boiling water to cover, then leave for about 1 minute. Drain, skin the tomatoes carefully and then roughly chop the flesh.

Heat the oil in a large saucepan, add the onion and fry for 5 minutes until softened and just beginning to brown. Stir in the garlic and pimentón and cook for a further 1 minute.

Stir in the tomatoes, red pepper, stock, wine and saffron. Add the bay leaves, season with salt and pepper and bring to the boil. Cover and simmer gently for 10 minutes, then remove the pan from the heat and set aside.

Discard any mussels that are open or have cracked shells. Scrub with a small nailbrush, remove any barnacles and pull off any small, hairy beards. Return the mussels to a bowl of clean water. Separate the squid tubes from the tentacles, then slice the tubes.

Reheat the tomato sauce if necessary, add the cod and the sliced squid and cook for 2 minutes. Drain the mussels and tip into the pan, cover with a tight-fitting lid and cook for 4 minutes. Add the squid tentacles and cook for a further 2 minutes until the fish is cooked through and all the mussels have opened. Gently stir, then serve, discarding any mussels that have not opened.

Green peppercorn steak

130 CALORIES PER SERVING

SERVES **2**

- 2 lean fillet steaks, about 75 g (3 oz) each
- ½ tablespoon green peppercorns in brine, drained
- 1 tablespoon light soy sauce
- ½ teaspoon balsamic vinegar
- 4 cherry tomatoes, halved
- thyme sprigs, to garnish

Heat a griddle pan until it is very hot, add the steaks and cook for 2–3 minutes on each side, then remove from the pan and keep warm.

Add the peppercorns, soy sauce, vinegar and tomatoes to the pan. Leave the liquids to sizzle for 2 minutes or until the tomatoe are soft. Spoon the sauce over the steaks and serve garnished with thyme sprigs.

Thai beef & pepper stir-fry

255 CALORIES PER SERVING

SERVES **4**

- 500 g (1 lb) lean beef fillet
- 1 tablespoon sesame oil
- 1 garlic clove, finely chopped
- 1 lemon grass stalk, finely shredded
- 2.5 cm (1 inch) piece of fresh root ginger, peeled and finely chopped
- 1 red pepper, cored, deseeded and thickly sliced
- 1 green pepper, cored, deseeded and thickly sliced
- 1 onion, thickly sliced
- 2 tablespoons lime juice
- pepper

Cut the beef into long, thin strips, cutting across the grain. Heat the oil in a wok or large frying pan over a high heat, add the garlic and stir-fry for 1 minute. Add the beef and stir-fry for 2–3 minutes until lightly coloured. Stir in the lemon grass and ginger and remove the pan from the heat. Remove the beef from the pan and set aside.

Add the peppers and onion to the pan and stir-fry for 2–3 minutes until the onions are just turning golden brown and are slightly softened. Return the beef to the pan, stir in the lime juice and season with pepper.

Russian meatballs

PREPARATION TIME **15 MINUTES, PLUS CHILLING** • COOKING TIME **ABOUT 1 HOUR**

154 CALORIES PER SERVING

SERVES **4**

- 375 g (12 oz) 5% fat minced beef
- 1 onion, roughly chopped
- 1 tablespoon tomato purée
- 1 teaspoon dried mixed herbs
- salt and pepper
- chopped parsley and parsley sprigs, to garnish
- mashed potato, to serve (optional)

Tomato sauce
- 1 red onion, finely chopped
- 400 g (13 oz) can chopped tomatoes
- pinch of paprika, plus extra to garnish
- 1 teaspoon dried mixed herbs

Place the beef, onion, tomato purée and dried mixed herbs in a blender or food processor. Season well with salt and pepper and blend until smooth. Shape the mixture into 12 balls and chill for 30 minutes.

Meanwhile, put all the tomato sauce ingredients in a saucepan and cook, uncovered, over a low heat for 15–20 minutes, stirring occasionally.

Season the sauce with salt and pepper and transfer to an ovenproof dish. Arrange the meatballs on top and place in a preheated oven, 180°C (350°F), Gas Mark 4, for 45 minutes. Sprinkle the meatballs with chopped parsley and paprika and garnished with parsley sprigs. Serve with mashed potato, if liked (remembering to count the calories).

Lean lasagne

PREPARATION TIME **30 MINUTES** • COOKING TIME **50–60 MINUTES**

340 CALORIES PER SERVING

SERVES 8

- 200 g (7 oz) pre-cooked sheets of lasagne
- pepper

Meat sauce
- 2 aubergines, peeled and diced
- 2 red onions, chopped
- 2 garlic cloves, crushed
- 300 ml (½ pint) vegetable stock
- 4 tablespoons red wine
- 500 g (1 lb) extra-lean minced beef
- 2 x 400 g (13 oz) cans chopped tomatoes

Cheese sauce
- 3 egg whites
- 250 g (8 oz) ricotta cheese
- 175 ml (6 fl oz) milk
- 6 tablespoons grated Parmesan cheese

To make the meat sauce, put the aubergines, onions, garlic, stock and wine in a large saucepan. Cover and simmer briskly for 5 minutes.

Remove the lid and cook for about a further 5 minutes until the aubergine is tender and the liquid is absorbed, adding a little more stock if necessary. Remove from the heat and leave to cool slightly, then purée in a blender or food processor.

Meanwhile, brown the beef in a nonstick frying pan. Skim off any fat. Add the aubergine mixture and tomatoes and season with pepper. Simmer briskly, uncovered, for about 10 minutes until thickened.

To make the cheese sauce, beat the egg whites with the ricotta in a bowl, then beat in the milk and 4 tablespoons of the Parmesan. Season with pepper.

Alternate layers of the meat sauce, lasagne and cheese sauce in an ovenproof dish, starting with meat sauce and finishing with cheese sauce. Sprinkle the top with the remaining Parmesan. Bake in a preheated oven, 180°C (350°F), Gas Mark 4, for 30–40 minutes until browned. Serve hot.

Lemon & caper pork tenderloin

PREPARATION TIME **20 MINUTES** • COOKING TIME **16–17 MINUTES**

320 CALORIES PER SERVING

SERVES **4**

- 2 thin pork tenderloins, about 300 g (10 oz) each, cut in half
- 1 garlic clove, roughly chopped
- 1 tablespoon chopped sage
- finely grated rind and juice of 1 lemon
- 4 teaspoons olive oil
- 2 teaspoons clear honey
- 1 tablespoon capers, drained
- 2 long banana shallots, chopped
- 300 g (10 oz) baby leaf spinach, roughly sliced
- salt and pepper
- 8–12 caperberries, to garnish

Slice the pork horizontally without quite cutting all the way through and open up each piece like a butterfly. Place the garlic, sage, lemon rind, 2 teaspoons of the oil, honey, capers and 1 teaspoon of the lemon juice in a mini food processor and blend to a rough paste. Rub the mixture all over the pork.

Heat a large nonstick frying pan over a medium heat, add the pork and fry for 1 minute to seal, turning once. Transfer the pork to a small roasting tin, season with salt and pepper and roast in a preheated oven, 220°C (425°F), Gas Mark 7, for 10 minutes or until cooked through and the juices run clear. Remove from the oven, cover with foil and leave to rest.

Meanwhile, heat the remaining oil in a frying pan over a low heat, add the shallots and cook for 5–6 minutes until softened. Add the spinach leaves to the pan and stir until wilted. Stir in the remaining lemon juice, season with salt and pepper, then spoon on to 4 serving plates. Place the pork on top and serve scattered with caperberries.

Pork skewers with coleslaw

PREPARATION TIME **25 MINUTES, PLUS MARINATING** • COOKING TIME **7–10 MINUTES**

296 CALORIES PER SERVING

SERVES **4**

- 600 g (1¼ lb) lean pork loin, cubed

Barbecue marinade
- 2 tablespoons muscovado sugar
- 2 tablespoons tomato ketchup
- 2 tablespoons dark soy sauce
- 1 teaspoon Chinese 5-spice powder
- 2 tablespoons orange juice

Coleslaw
- 1 tablespoon red wine vinegar
- 2 teaspoons piri-piri sauce or marinade
- ½ teaspoon granulated sugar
- 4–6 tablespoons extra-light mayonnaise
- ½ red cabbage, shredded
- 2 carrots, grated
- 2 spring onions, thinly sliced
- salt and pepper

Mix together the marinade ingredients in a large non-metallic bowl until smooth. Add the pork and mix until well coated. Leave to marinate for 15 minutes.

Meanwhile, make the coleslaw. Mix together the vinegar, piri-piri sauce, sugar and mayonnaise in a small bowl. Toss the cabbage, carrots and spring onions together in a large bowl, then add the dressing and mix together until well combined. Season with salt and pepper and set aside.

Thread the pork on to 8 metal skewers and cook under a preheated grill for 7–10 minutes, turning occasionally, until cooked through and sticky. Serve 2 skewers per person with the coleslaw.

Herby lamb with butter beans

PREPARATION TIME **15 MINUTES, PLUS CHILLING** • COOKING TIME **10 MINUTES**

305 CALORIES PER SERVING

SERVES **4**

2 tablespoons finely
chopped mint
1 tablespoon finely
chopped thyme
1 tablespoon finely
chopped oregano
½ tablespoon finely
chopped rosemary
4 teaspoons wholegrain
mustard
4 lamb noisettes, about
125 g (4 oz) each

Tangy butter beans
2 teaspoons sunflower oil
1 onion, chopped
250 g (8 oz) cooked butter
beans or drained canned
beans
1 tablespoon tomato purée
50 ml (2 fl oz) pineapple
juice
2 tablespoons lemon juice
a few drops of Tabasco
sauce
pepper

Mix together all the chopped herbs in a bowl. Spread mustard on both sides of each noisette and dip the meat into the herb mixture. Press the herbs firmly to the mustard. Chill the lamb until you are ready to cook.

To make the tangy butter beans, heat the oil in a frying pan, add the onion and fry until softened. Add the remaining ingredients and cook gently for 5 minutes.

Meanwhile, cook the lamb noisettes under a preheated hot grill for about 4 minutes on each side until cooked but still slightly pink in the centre. Serve immediately with the butter beans.

TOP TIP

Plan your fasting days at the beginning of the week. It is a good idea to fast on days when you will be busy as won't have so much time to think about food if you have a long list of things to get through.

Lamb & flageolet bean stew

PREPARATION TIME **10 MINUTES** • COOKING TIME **1 HOUR 20 MINUTES**

288 CALORIES PER SERVING

SERVES **4**

- 1 teaspoon olive oil
- 350 g (11½ oz) lean lamb, cubed
- 16 pickling onions, peeled
- 1 garlic clove, crushed
- 1 tablespoon plain flour
- 600 ml (1 pint) lamb stock
- 200 g (7 oz) can chopped tomatoes
- 1 bouquet garni
- 2 x 400 g (13 oz) cans flageolet beans, rinsed and drained
- 250 g (8 oz) cherry tomatoes
- pepper

Heat the oil in a flameproof casserole or saucepan, add the lamb and fry for 3-4 minutes until browned all over. Remove from the casserole and set aside.

Add the onions and garlic to the pan and fry for 4–5 minutes until the onions are beginning to brown.

Return the lamb and any juices to the pan, then stir through the flour and add the stock, canned tomatoes, bouquet garni and beans. Bring to the boil, stirring, then cover and simmer for 1 hour until the lamb is just tender.

Add the cherry tomatoes to the pan, season well with pepper and simmer for a further 10 minutes, then serve hot.

TOP TIP

Try drinking green tea. It contains no calories, is rich in antioxidants and may even marginally increase your metabolic rate, giving you a slight weight loss advantage.

Turkish lamb & potato stew

PREPARATION TIME **20 MINUTES** • COOKING TIME **2–2¼ HOURS**

307 CALORIES PER SERVING

SERVES 6

- 375 g (12 oz) tomatoes
- 1 tablespoon vegetable oil
- 500 g (1 lb) lean lamb, cut into 1.5 cm (¾ inch) cubes
- 4 onions, cut into wedges
- 2 garlic cloves, crushed
- 750 g (1½ lb) potatoes, peeled and cut into chunks
- 1 red or green pepper, cored, deseeded and sliced
- 900 ml (1½ pints) stock or water
- 2 tablespoons wine vinegar
- 2 bay leaves
- 1 teaspoon chopped sage
- 1 tablespoon chopped dill or fennel leaves
- 1 aubergine and/or 1 trimmed and chopped fennel bulb
- 12 pitted black olives
- pepper

Put the tomatoes in a large saucepan or heatproof bowl and pour over enough boiling water to cover, then leave for about 1 minute. Drain, skin the tomatoes carefully and then quarter or slice the flesh.

Heat the oil in a large, heavy-based saucepan, add the lamb and fry, stirring, until sealed and browned all over.

Add the onions and garlic and fry gently for about 5 minutes until softened. Add the potatoes, tomatoes, pepper, stock or water and vinegar and bring to the boil. Add the herbs and season well with pepper. Cover and simmer gently for 1 hour.

Stir well, then add the aubergine and/or fennel and olives. Bring back to the boil, cover and simmer gently for 45–60 minutes until the lamb is very tender, stirring occasionally. Discard the bay leaves before serving.

Veal with lemon

PREPARATION TIME **10 MINUTES** • COOKING TIME **40–45 MINUTES**

368 CALORIES PER SERVING

SERVES 4

- 2 tablespoons olive oil
- 1 kg (2 lb) veal, cubed
- 2 onions, sliced
- 4 garlic cloves, sliced
- 2 baby fennel bulbs, trimmed and roughly chopped
- 475 ml (16 fl oz) white wine
- 475 ml (16 fl oz) chicken stock
- rind of ½ lemon, cut into matchsticks
- 4 bay leaves
- 1 tablespoon thyme leaves
- salt and pepper

Heat the oil in a large frying pan over a high heat, add the veal and brown evenly. Remove from the pan with a slotted spoon and set aside.

Add the onion and garlic to the pan and cook over a medium heat until golden. Add the fennel and fry for a further 3–4 minutes or until softened.

Return the veal to the pan and add the wine, stock, lemon rind, bay leaves and thyme. Bring to the boil and boil for 5 minutes. Reduce the heat, cover and simmer for a further 20–25 minutes. Season and serve hot.

TOP TIP

Reward yourself for your successes. Set yourself targets and, once you have reached them, treat yourself to something nice.

Calves' liver with garlic mash

PREPARATION TIME **10 MINUTES** • COOKING TIME **12–16 MINUTES**

393 CALORIES PER SERVING

SERVES 2

350 g (¾ lb) potatoes, peeled and cubed

1 garlic clove

3 tablespoons light crème fraîche

½ tablespoon chopped sage

2 slices of calves liver, about 150 g (5 oz) each

1 tablespoon seasoned flour

½ tablespoon olive oil

salt and pepper

gravy, to serve

Cook the potatoes and garlic in a saucepan of lightly salted boiling water for 10–12 minutes until tender, then drain. Return the potatoes and garlic to the pan and mash with the crème fraîche and sage. Season well with pepper.

Meanwhile, press the pieces of liver into the seasoned flour to coat them all over. Heat the oil in a frying pan, add the liver and fry for 1–2 minutes on each side or until cooked to your liking. Serve with the mash and gravy.

Orangey baked nectarines

PREPARATION TIME **5 MINUTES** • COOKING TIME **18–20 MINUTES**

161 CALORIES PER SERVING

SERVES 2

- 25 ml (1 fl oz) orange liqueur, such as Cointreau
- ½ teaspoon vanilla bean paste or extract
- finely grated rind of ¼ orange
- 1 tablespoon clear honey
- 2 firm, ripe nectarines, halved and stoned
- 75 g (3 oz) 0% Greek yogurt with honey, to serve

Put the orange liqueur, vanilla bean paste or extract, orange rind and honey in a bowl and stir until well combined.

Arrange the nectarines, cut side up, in an ovenproof dish, then drizzle over the liqueur mixture. Bake in a preheated oven, 180°C (350°F), Gas Mark 4, for 18–20 minutes until tender.

Divide the nectarines among 2 serving bowls and serve with the yogurt, drizzled with any juices from the pan.

Creole pineapple wedges

PREPARATION TIME **10 MINUTES** • COOKING TIME **8–10 MINUTES**

159
CALORIES
PER SERVING

SERVES
4

- 1 small pineapple, about 1.25 kg (2½ lb)
- 1 tablespoon dark rum
- juice of 1 lime
- 15 g (½ oz) sesame seeds

Cut the pineapple lengthways, first in half and then into quarters, leaving the leaves intact. The wedges should be about 1 cm (½ inch) thick, so it may be necessary to divide the quarters again.

Mix together the dark rum and lime juice in a bowl and sprinkle the mixture over the pineapple slices.

Toast the pineapple under a preheated hot grill for 8–10 minutes, turning to ensure even cooking. Serve immediately, sprinkled with the sesame seeds.

Bananas en papillote

PREPARATION TIME **5 MINUTES** • COOKING TIME **3–4 MINUTES**

95 CALORIES PER SERVING

SERVES **4**

- butter, for greasing
- 4 small, firm bananas
- 1 cinnamon stick, cut into 4
- 4 star anise
- 1 vanilla pod, cut into 4
- 2 tablespoons grated dark chocolate
- 75 ml (3 fl oz) pineapple juice

Lightly grease 4 pieces of foil or nonstick baking paper, each large enough to wrap a banana.

Place a banana in the centre of each piece and add a piece of cinnamon stick, 1 star anise and a piece of vanilla pod to each. Sprinkle over the grated chocolate and pineapple juice. Fold up the parcels and seal to make airtight pockets.

Place the parcels on a baking sheet and bake in a preheated oven, 230°C (450°F), Gas Mark 8, for 3–4 minutes. Alternatively cook on top of a barbecue or by the side of a bonfire – in both cases use double-thickness aluminium foil to prevent splits and spillages. Serve warm.

Peach consommé with raspberries

PREPARATION TIME **10 MINUTES, PLUS CHILLING** • COOKING TIME **20 MINUTES**

124 CALORIES PER SERVING

SERVES 4

600 ml (1 pint) water
1 vanilla pod
1 star anise
1 cinnamon stick
3 tablespoons honey
8 peaches
juice of 1 lemon

To decorate
150 g (5 oz) raspberries
mint sprigs

Put the measurement water, vanilla pod, star anise, cinnamon stick and honey in a large saucepan. Bring to the boil and simmer for 5 minutes. Add the peaches and poach for 5 minutes, then remove 4 of them with a slotted spoon and leave to cool.

Add the lemon juice to the reserved liquid and simmer the remaining peaches for a further 10 minutes until mushy.

Meanwhile, gently peel the skins away from the cooled peaches and chill in the refrigerator.

Remove the stones from the mushy peaches and blend the pulp and cooking liquid in a blender or food processor. Push the purée through a fine sieve and chill.

When ready to serve, place 1 poached peach in each of 4 serving bowls and pour one-quarter of the fruit consommé over the top of each. Decorate with the raspberries and sprigs of mint and serve.

Apple & berry strudels

PREPARATION TIME **7 MINUTES** • COOKING TIME **20 MINUTES**

102 CALORIES PER SERVING

SERVES **4**

- 2 cooking apples, peeled and grated
- 175 g (6 oz) mixed berries
- pinch of ground cinnamon
- 1 tablespoon clear honey
- 2 sheets of filo pastry
- 1 egg white
- mint sprigs, to decorate
- low-fat custard, to serve (optional)

Put the grated apples, berries, cinnamon and 1 teaspoon of the honey in a saucepan and cook gently for about 5 minutes or until the fruit is soft.

Brush the filo sheets with egg white and place 1 sheet on top of the other. Cut the sheets into quarters and place one-quarter of the fruit in the centre of each rectangle. Tuck in the ends of the pastry and roll into sausage shapes.

Place the strudels on a baking sheet, brush with the remaining honey and bake in a preheated oven, 150°C (300°F), Gas Mark for 15 minutes or until golden brown.

Decorate the strudels with sprigs of mint and serve with a little low-fat custard, if liked (remembering to count the calories).

Chinese spiced citrus salad

PREPARATION TIME 15 MINUTES, PLUS INFUSING AND CHILLING • COOKING TIME 5 MINUTES

163 CALORIES PER SERVING

SERVES 4

3 oranges, peeled and pith removed, separated into segments
1 ruby grapefruit, peeled and pith removed, separated into segments
1 banana, thinly sliced
150 g (5 oz) low-fat crème fraîche, to serve

Syrup
1 whole clove
¼ teaspoon Chinese 5-spice powder
rind of 1 lime
1 vanilla pod, split lengthways
¼ teaspoon peeled and grated fresh root ginger
300 ml (½ pint) water

To decorate
1 tablespoon finely chopped mint
seeds of 1 pomegranate

To make the syrup, combine all the ingredients in a saucepan, bring to the boil and simmer gently for 3–5 minutes. Remove the pan from the heat and leave the syrup to infuse and cool.

Meanwhile, mix together the orange and grapefruit segments in an attractive glass serving bowl. Add the banana slices.

Pour the cooled syrup through a sieve to remove the solids, then pour it over the fruits. Cover and chill for 2–3 hours.

Divide the fruit salad among 4 serving bowls, top with the crème fraîche and serve decorated with the mint and pomegranate seeds.

TOP TIP

The average food craving lasts about 10 minutes, so try to distract yourself to get past your hunger pang. Make yourself a cup of herbal tea, have a bath or phone a friend.

Honeyed figs

PREPARATION TIME **5 MINUTES** • COOKING TIME **2–3 MINUTES**

132 CALORIES PER SERVING

SERVES **4**

- 8 fresh figs, preferably black, halved
- 1 tablespoon clear honey
- 75 g (3 oz) goats' cheese, cut into 4 thin slices
- 125 g (4 oz) raspberries
- handful of flat leaf parsley, chopped, to decorate

Put the figs, cut side up, in a foil-lined grill pan and drizzle a little honey into the centre of each. Cook under a preheated hot grill for 2–3 minutes.

Transfer to 4 serving plates and serve hot with the goats' cheese and raspberries, sprinkled with the parsley.

Mango & passion fruit trifle

PREPARATION TIME **10 MINUTES, PLUS CHILLING**

171 CALORIES PER SERVING

SERVES **2**

- 2 sponge fingers
- 75 g (3 oz) 0% Greek yogurt
- 100 g (3½ oz) half-fat crème fraîche
- 2 passion fruit
- ½ mango, peeled, stoned and diced

Break each sponge finger into 4 pieces an divide among 2 tumblers. Mix together th yogurt and crème fraîche in a bowl.

Halve the passion fruit and remove the seeds. Spoon the seeds over the fingers, then add half of the mango pieces.

Pour half the crème fraîche mixture over the fruit, then top with the remaining mango. Spoon over the remaining crème fraîche and top with the remaining passio fruit. Chill for 1 hour before serving.

Mango & clementine sorbet

PREPARATION TIME 20 MINUTES, PLUS COOLING AND FREEZING • COOKING TIME 5 MINUTES

95 CALORIES PER SERVING

SERVES 6

200 ml (7 fl oz) water
50 g (2 oz) light brown sugar
500 g (1 lb) clementines, about 7 in total, halved
2 large mangoes, stoned and peeled
1 egg white
grated rind and juice of 1 lime

Put the measurement water in a small saucepan and add the sugar. Gently bring to the boil and heat until the sugar has dissolved. Remove the pan from the heat and leave the syrup to cool.

Squeeze the juice from the clementines. Purée the flesh of 1 of the mangoes until it is smooth. Stir the mango purée and clementine juice into the cooled sugar syrup and mix together.

Pour the mixture into a plastic container, cover and freeze for 2–3 hours until semi-frozen. Beat well with a fork or blitz in a food processor to break up the ice crystals, then repeat the freezing and beating process. Mix in the egg white, then freeze until solid.

Alternatively, churn the mixture in an ice-cream maker for 20–30 minutes until the sorbet is thick. Add the egg white and continue churning until the sorbet is well mixed and thick enough to scoop. Serve immediately or transfer to a plastic container and store in the freezer until required.

Take the sorbet out of the freezer and leave to soften at room temperature for 15 minutes before serving. Slice the remaining mango and toss the slices in the lime juice and rind mixture. Scoop the sorbet into 6 serving dishes and serve with the mango slices.

Champagne granita

PREPARATION TIME **20 MINUTES, PLUS COOLING AND FREEZING** • COOKING TIME **5 MINUTES**

80 CALORIES PER SERVING

SERVES 6

- 150 ml (¼ pint) water
- 40 g (1½ oz) light brown sugar
- 375 ml (13 fl oz) medium-dry champagne
- 150 g (5 oz) alpine or wild strawberries

Put the measurement water in a small saucepan and add the sugar. Gently bring to the boil and heat until the sugar has dissolved. Remove the pan from the heat and leave the syrup to cool.

Mix together the cooled sugar syrup and champagne, then pour the mixture into a shallow, nonstick baking tin so that it is no more than 2.5 cm (1 inch) deep.

Freeze the mixture for 2 hours until it is mushy, then break up the ice crystals with a fork. Return the mixture to the freezer for a further 2 hours, beating every 30 minutes until it has formed fine, icy flakes.

To serve, spoon the granita and the strawberries into 6 dessert glasses and serve immediately.

Coconut & lime ice cream

PREPARATION TIME **20 MINUTES, PLUS COOLING AND FREEZING** • COOKING TIME **5 MINUTES**

168 CALORIES PER SERVING

SERVES **4**

- 150 ml (¼ pint) water
- 75 g (3 oz) light brown sugar
- 6 dried kaffir lime leaves
- finely grated rind of 1 lemon
- 400 ml (14 fl oz) can reduced-fat coconut milk
- lemon or lime rind curls, to decorate

Put the measurement water in a small saucepan and add the sugar. Gently bring to the boil and heat until the sugar has dissolved. Remove the pan from the heat and add the lime leaves, then cover and leave the syrup to cool and infuse for at least 2 hours.

Remove the lime leaves from the cooled syrup and reserve. Mix the syrup with the lemon rind and coconut milk.

Pour the mixture into a plastic container, cover and freeze for 6–8 hours, beating 2 or 3 times with a fork to break up the ice crystals.

Alternatively, churn the mixture in an ice-cream maker for 20–30 minutes until thick and spoonable. Serve immediately, or transfer to a plastic container and store in the freezer until required.

Take the ice cream out of the freezer and leave to soften at room temperature for 15 minutes before serving. Scoop the ice cream into 4 small glasses and serve decorated with the reserved lime leaves.

Chocolate orange soufflés

PREPARATION TIME **10 MINUTES** • COOKING TIME **11–14 MINUTES**

178 CALORIES PER SERVING

SERVES 6

- 75 ml (3 fl oz) orange juice
- 75 g (3 oz) caster sugar
- 4 large egg whites
- 25 g (1 oz) unsweetened cocoa powder
- 2 tablespoons orange liqueur
- vegetable oil, for greasing
- 125 g (4 oz) low-fat vanilla ice cream, softened

Put the orange juice and sugar in a small saucepan and heat for 3–4 minutes over a medium-high heat, stirring occasionally until the mixture has a syrupy consistency. Remove the pan from the heat.

In a large, clean bowl, whisk the egg whites until stiff, but stop before dry peaks form. Pour the syrup over the egg whites and beat for 2 minutes. Add the cocoa powder and liqueur and beat briefly until well mixed.

Pour the mixture into 6 lightly greased ovenproof cups and bake in a preheated oven, 220°C (425°F), Gas Mark 7, for 8–10 minutes or until the soufflés are puffed. Do not overcook or the soufflés will become tough.

Spoon 2 tablespoons of the softened ice cream into the centre of each soufflé and serve immediately.

Pimm's jellies

PREPARATION TIME **20 MINUTES, PLUS CHILLING** • COOKING TIME **4–5 MINUTES**

85 CALORIES PER SERVING

SERVES **6**

- 3 tablespoons water
- 3 teaspoons powdered gelatine
- 1 dessert apple, cored and diced
- 1 tablespoon lemon juice
- 250 g (8 oz) strawberries, hulled and sliced
- 1 peach, halved, stoned and diced
- 1 orange, peeled and cut into segments
- 150 ml (¼ pint) Pimm's No. 1
- 450 ml (¾ pint) diet lemonade, chilled

To decorate
- peach slices
- strawberries, hulled and halved
- mint sprigs or borage flowers
- orange rind curls

Put the measurement water in a small, heatproof bowl and sprinkle the gelatine over the top, making sure that all the powder is absorbed by the water. Leave to soak for 5 minutes. Stand the bowl in a small saucepan of gently simmering water so that the water comes halfway up the sides of the bowl. Heat for 4–5 minutes until the gelatine has dissolved and the liquid is clear.

Meanwhile, put the apple pieces in a bowl and toss with the lemon juice. Add the other fruits, mix together and divide among 6 glasses.

Stir the gelatine into the Pimm's and slowly mix in the lemonade. Pour the mixture over the fruit in the glasses. Transfer the jellies to the refrigerator and leave to chill and set for at least 4 hours.

Before serving, decorate the tops of the glasses with peach slices, strawberry halves, mint sprigs or borage flowers and orange rind curls. To make orange rind curls, use a canelle knife to pare away the rind in strips, then wrap the strips tightly around a skewer or the handle of a wooden spoon. Slide them off after a minute or two.

Mango & passion fruit brûlées

PREPARATION TIME **10 MINUTES, PLUS CHILLING** • COOKING TIME **1–2 MINUTES**

131 CALORIES PER SERVING

SERVES 2

- ½ small mango, peeled, stoned and thinly sliced
- 1 passion fruit, halved and flesh scooped out
- 150 g (5 oz) low-fat natural yogurt
- 100 g (3½ oz) crème fraîche
- ½ tablespoon icing sugar
- a few drops of vanilla essence
- 1 tablespoon demerara sugar

Divide the mango slices between 2 ramekins.

Mix together the passion fruit flesh, yogurt, crème fraîche, icing sugar and vanilla essence in a bowl, then spoon the mixture over the mango. Tap each ramekin to level the surface.

Sprinkle over the demerara sugar, then cook the brûlées under a preheated hot grill for 1–2 minutes until the sugar has melted. Chill for about 30 minutes before serving.

Brûlée vanilla cheesecake

PREPARATION TIME **30 MINUTES, PLUS COOLING AND CHILLING** • COOKING TIME **30–35 MINUTES**

160 CALORIES PER SERVING

SERVES **6**

- 600 g (1¼ lb) less than 1% fat soft cheese (quark)
- 6 tablespoons granulated sweetener
- 1½ teaspoons vanilla essence
- finely grated rind of ½ orange
- 4 eggs, separated
- butter, for greasing
- 1 tablespoon icing sugar, sifted
- 3 oranges, peeled and cut into segments

Mix together the cheese, sweetener, vanilla essence, orange rind and egg yolks in a bowl until smooth.

In a large, clean bowl, whisk the egg whites until softly peaking, then fold a large spoonful into the cheese mixture to loosen it. Add the remaining egg whites and gently fold them in.

Pour the mixture into a greased 20 cm (8 inch) springform cake tin and level the surface. Bake in a preheated oven, 160°C (325°F), Gas Mark 3, for 30–35 minutes until well risen, golden brown and just set in the centre.

Turn off the oven and leave the cheesecake inside to cool for 15 minutes with the door slightly ajar. Remove from the oven, leave to cool, then chill in the refrigerator for 4 hours. (The cheesecake sinks slightly as it cools.)

Run a knife around the cheesecake, loosen the tin and transfer to a serving plate. Dust the top with the sifted icing sugar and caramelize the sugar with a cook's blowtorch. Serve within 30 minutes, while the sugar topping is still hard and brittle. Cut into 6 wedges and serve with the orange segments.

Passion fruit panna cotta

PREPARATION TIME **15 MINUTES, PLUS COOLING AND CHILLING** • COOKING TIME **5 MINUTES**

144 CALORIES PER SERVING

SERVES **2**

1 gelatine leaf
4 passion fruit
100 g (3½ oz) half-fat
crème fraîche
50 g (2 oz) 0% Greek
yogurt
50 ml (2 fl oz) water
½ teaspoon caster sugar
½ vanilla pod, split
lengthways

Soften the gelatine leaves in cold water.

Halve the passion fruit and remove the seeds, working over a bowl to catch the juice. Reserve the seeds for decoration. Mix together the crème fraîche and yogurt with the passion fruit juice.

Put the measurement water in a saucepan, add the sugar and scrape in the vanilla pod seeds, then heat gently, stirring, until the sugar has dissolved. Drain the gelatin and add to the pan. Leave to cool.

Mix the gelatine mixture into the crème fraîche mixture, then pour into 2 ramekins or moulds. Cover and chill for 6 hours or until set. Turn the panna cotta out of the moulds on to serving plates by briefly immersing in hot water. Spoon over the reserved seeds and serve.

Strawberry roulade

PREPARATION TIME **30 MINUTES, PLUS COOLING** • COOKING TIME **8 MINUTES**

110 CALORIES PER SERVING

SERVES 8

- vegetable oil, for greasing
- 3 eggs
- 125 g (4 oz) caster sugar
- 125 g (4 oz) plain flour, sifted
- 1 tablespoon hot water
- 500 g (1 lb) fresh strawberries, hulled and quartered or 425 g (14 oz) can strawberries in natural juice, drained and quartered
- 200 g (7 oz) natural fromage frais or yogurt
- icing sugar, for dusting

Lightly grease a 33 x 23 cm (13 x 9 inch) Swiss roll tin. Line with greaseproof paper to come about 1 cm (½ inch) above the sides of the tin. Lightly grease the paper.

Whisk the eggs and sugar in a large bowl over a saucepan of hot water until pale and thick. Fold the flour into the egg mixture with the measurement water. Pour the mixture into the prepared tin and bake in a preheated oven, 220°C (425°F), Gas Mark 7, for 8 minutes until golden and set.

Meanwhile, place a sheet of greaseproof paper 2.5 cm (1 inch) larger all round than the Swiss roll tin on a clean, damp tea towel. Once cooked, immediately turn out the Swiss roll face down on to the paper. Carefully peel off the lining paper. Roll the sponge up tightly with the new greaseproof paper inside. Wrap the tea towel around the outside and place on a wire rack until cool, then unroll carefully.

Add half the strawberries to the fromage frais or yogurt and spread over the sponge. Roll the sponge up again and trim the ends. Dust with icing sugar and decorate with a few strawberries.

Purée the remaining strawberries in a blender or food processor. Cut the roulade into 8 slices and serve with the strawberry sauce.

Plum & ricotta almond cake

PREPARATION TIME **30 MINUTES, PLUS COOLING AND CHILLING** • COOKING TIME **35–40 MINUTES**

150 CALORIES PER SERVING

SERVES **6**

butter, for greasing
500 g (1 lb) sweet, ripe red plums, stoned and quartered
250 g (8 oz) ricotta cheese
4–5 tablespoons granulated sweetener
3 eggs, separated
¼ teaspoon almond extract
4 teaspoons flaked almonds
2 tablespoons water
1 tablespoon icing sugar, sifted

Arrange half the plums randomly over the base of a greased and base-lined 20 cm (8 inch) springform cake tin.

Mix together the ricotta, 4 tablespoons of the sweetener, the egg yolks and almond extract in a bowl until smooth. In a separate clean bowl, whisk the egg whites until stiff, moist peaks form. Fold into the ricotta mixture, then spoon over the plums.

Sprinkle the top with the flaked almonds and bake in a preheated oven, 160°C (325°F), Gas Mark 3, for 30–35 minutes until the cake is well risen, golden brown and the centre is just set. Check after 20 minutes and cover the top loosely with foil if the almonds seem to be browning too quickly.

Turn off the oven and leave the cake to cool for 15 minutes with the door slightly ajar. Remove from the oven, leave to cool, then chill well in the refrigerator.

Meanwhile, put the remaining plums and measurement water in a saucepan, cover and cook for 5 minutes until soft. Purée in a blender or food processor until smooth, mix in the remaining sweetener if needed, then pour into a small jug.

To serve, remove the tin and lining paper and transfer the cake to a serving plate. Dust the top with the sifted icing sugar and serve, cut into 6 wedges, with the sauce.

Calorie counter

FRUIT	Average portion (g)	Calories
Apples (weighed whole with core)		
Cox's Pippin	125	53
Golden Delicious	125	50
Granny Smith	125	52
Apples (stewed with sugar)	110	81
Apricots (flesh only)	80	25
Avocado (flesh only)	140	266
Bananas	100	95
Blackberries	100	25
Blueberries	50	35
Cherries (weighed with stones)	80	31
Clementines (weighed with peel and pips)	80	22
Figs	55	24
Fruit Salad	140	77
Grapefruit (weighed with peel and pips)	170	20
Grapes	100	60
Kiwifruit (weighed with skin)	75	32
Lemon, unpeeled	60	8
Lime, unpeeled	40	4
Melon (weighed with skin)		
Cantaloupe	180	23
Galia	200	30
Honeydew	200	38
Nectarines (weighed with skin)	150	54
Oranges (weighed with skin)	200	52
Papaya (flesh only)	140	50
Peaches (weighed with stone)	150	45
Pears (weighed whole with core)	150	54
Pineapple	80	33
Plums (weighed with stone)	70	24
Raspberries	60	15
Satsumas (weighed with skin)	87	23
Strawberries	100	27
Watermelon (flesh only)	200	62

DRIED FRUIT, NUTS AND SEEDS		
Almonds	15	91
Apricots, dried	32	60
Brazil Nuts	10	68
Cashew Nuts	10	63
Cashew Nuts, roasted and salted	25	153
Chestnuts	50	85
Cranberries, dried, sweetened	25	82
Dates, dried, pitted	50	35
Figs, ready-to-eat	20	68
Hazelnuts	10	65
Mixed Nuts	40	243
Mixed Nuts and Raisins	40	192
Peanuts, plain	13	73
Peanuts, dry-roasted	40	236
Pecan Nuts	20	138
Pine Nuts	5	34
Pistachio Nuts, roasted and salted	10	60
Prunes, dried	66	93
Pumpkin Seeds	16	91
Raisins, seedless	25	76
Sultanas	25	73
Sunflower Seeds	16	96
Walnuts	20	138

VEGETABLES (RAW, PREPARED, UNLESS OTHERWISE STATED)	Average portion (g)	Calories
Asparagus	125	33
Aubergine (grilled)	100	75
Beans		
Broad	120	58
French	90	20
Runner	90	16
Beetroot	40	18
Broccoli	85	20
Brussels Sprouts	90	32
Cabbage		
Red	90	14
Savoy	95	16
White	95	13
Carrots	60	14
Cauliflower	90	25
Celery	30	2
Chilli Peppers	10	3
Corn on the Cob (weighed whole)	200	123
Courgettes	90	17
Cucumber	23	2
Fennel	100	11
Leeks	75	16
Lettuce	80	13
Mushrooms	80	10
Onions	150	54
Parsnips	65	43
Peas	70	55
Peppers		
Green	160	24
Red	160	51
Yellow	160	42
Potatoes		
New (boiled)	175	116
Old (baked)	180	245
Old (boiled)	175	126
Old (mashed with butter)	120	122
Old (roasted)	130	151
Radishes	48	6
Spinach	90	23
Spring Onions	10	2
Squash (baked)	65	21
Swede	60	7
Sweet Potato (baked)	130	150
Sweetcorn	60	14
Tomatoes	85	14
Tomatoes (grilled)	85	42
Tomatoes, Cherry	90	16

CHEESE		
Brie	40	144
Camembert	40	116
Cheddar	40	166
Cheese Spread	30	81
Cottage, 4% fat	40	36
Cottage, 2% fat	40	28
Danish Blue	30	103
Dolcelatte	40	158
Double Gloucester	40	165
Edam	40	136
Emmental	40	160
Feta	50	125

	Average portion (g)	Calories
ouda	40	151
alloumi	40	124
ozzarella, fresh	55	141
ozzarella, grated	55	164
aneer	40	130
armesan, freshly grated	20	82
ed Leicester	40	161
icotta	55	79
oquefort	28	105
oft light	30	47
oft medium fat	30	74
ilton	35	143

GGS

	Average portion (g)	Calories
oiled	50	74
ried	60	107
oached	50	74
melette, Cheese (2 eggs)	150	399
melette, Plain (2 eggs)	120	180
melette, Spanish (2 eggs)	150	229
crambled, no milk (2 eggs)	100	160
crambled, with milk (2 eggs)	120	296

AIRY

	Average portion (g)	Calories
rème fraîche	50	190
rème fraîche, low fat	50	85
romage frais, fruit	100	135
romage frais, fruit, virtually fat-free	100	50
romage frais, natural	100	113
romage frais, natural, virtually fat-free	100	48
reek Yogurt, 0%	100	57
ilk		
Goats' Milk	146	88
Semi-skimmed Milk	146	67
Skimmed Milk	146	48
Soya Milk	146	47
Whole Milk	146	96

EAT

	Average portion (g)	Calories
eef		
Braising Steak (braised)	140	315
Braising Steak (slow-cooked)	140	276
Fillet Steak (grilled)	168	316
Mince, extra lean (stewed)	140	248
Rump Steak (grilled)	163	287
Rump Steak strips (stir-fried)	103	214
Sirloin Steak (grilled)	166	292
amb		
Leg Steaks (grilled)	90	178
Loin Chops (grilled)	70	149
Mince (stewed)	90	187
Rack of Lamb (roasted)	90	203
Shoulder Joint (roasted)	90	212
Stewing (stewed)	130	312
ffal		
Liver, Lambs' (fried)	100	237
Liver, Ox (stewed)	70	139
Liver, Pig (stewed)	70	132
Livers, Chicken (fried)	70	118
ork, Bacon and Ham		
Bacon		
Collar Joint (boiled)	46	88

	Average portion (g)	Calories
Loin Steaks (grilled)	100	191
Rashers, Back (dry-fried)	100	295
Rashers, Back (grilled)	100	214
Rashers, Back, dry-cured (grilled)	100	257
Rashers, Back, smoked (grilled)	100	293
Rashers, Back, sweet cure (grilled)	100	258
Rashers, Middle (grilled)	100	307
Rashers, Streaky (grilled)	100	337
Fillet of Pork (grilled)	120	240
Gammon		
Joint (boiled)	170	347
Rashers (grilled)	100	199
Ham		
Ham, Parma	47	105
Ham, premium	56	74
Pork Shoulder, cured	100	103
Leg Joint (roasted)	90	164
Loin Chops (grilled)	75	140
Loin Joint (pot-roasted)	90	177
Loin Steaks (fried)	120	229
Mince (stewed)	90	172
Pork, diced (stewed)	90	166
Pork Steaks (grilled)	135	228
Spare Rib (grilled)	110	321
Spare Rib Joint (pot-roasted)	90	181

POULTRY AND GAME

	Average portion (g)	Calories
Chicken		
Breast, skinless (grilled)	130	192
Breast strips (stir-fried)	90	145
Drumsticks, skinned (casseroled)	47	87
Drumsticks, skinned (roasted)	47	71
Leg Quarter (roasted)	146	345
Leg Quarter, skinned (casseroled)	146	257
Thighs, skinless, boneless (casseroled)	45	81
Wings (grilled)	100	274
Duck (roasted)	185	361
Goose (roasted)	185	590
Grouse (roasted)	160	205
Pheasant (roasted)	160	352
Pigeon (roasted)	115	215
Rabbit (stewed)	160	182
Turkey		
Breast, skinless (grilled)	90	140
Drumsticks, skinned (roasted)	90	146
Mince (stewed)	90	158
Strips (stir-fried)	90	148
Thighs, diced skinless, boneless (casseroled)	90	163
Venison (roasted)	120	198

FISH AND SEAFOOD

	Average portion (g)	Calories
Anchovies, in oil	10	28
Cod (baked)	120	115
Cod (poached)	120	113
Cod (steamed)	120	100
Cod, Smoked (poached)	120	121
Crab (boiled, dressed in shell)	130	166
Crab, in brine	40	31
Haddock (grilled)	120	125
Haddock (poached)	120	136
Haddock (steamed)	120	107
Haddock, Smoked (poached)	150	201

	Average portion (g)	Calories
Hake (grilled)	100	113
Halibut (grilled)	145	175
Halibut (poached)	110	169
Halibut (steamed)	110	144
Kipper (baked)	130	267
Kipper (grilled)	130	332
Lobster (boiled, dressed in shell)	250	258
Mackerel (grilled)	147	351
Monkfish (grilled)	70	67
Mussels (boiled, shelled)	40	42
Plaice (grilled)	130	125
Prawns (boiled, shelled)	60	59
Salmon (grilled)	82	176
Salmon (steamed)	77	152
Salmon, Smoked	56	80
Sardines (grilled)	40	78
Scallops (steamed, shelled)	70	83
Swordfish (grilled)	125	174
Trout, Brown (steamed)	155	209
Trout, Rainbow (steamed)	155	209
Tuna, canned in brine	45	45
Tuna, raw	45	61

RICE, PASTA AND PULSES (UNCOOKED, UNLESS OTHERWISE STATED)

	Average portion (g)	Calories
Bulgar Wheat	100	338
Butter Beans, canned	100	77
Butter Beans, dried (boiled)	100	103
Cannellini Beans, canned	100	87
Chickpeas, canned	100	115
Chickpeas, dried (boiled)	100	121
Couscous	100	364
Lentils, Puy-style, canned	100	118
Lentils, Puy-style, dried (boiled)	100	105
Kidney Beans, canned	100	100
Macaroni (boiled)	125	108
Noodles, Egg (boiled)	125	78
Noodles (fried)	125	191
Rice		
Brown (boiled)	125	176
White, glutinous (boiled)	125	82
White, polished (boiled)	125	154
Spaghetti (boiled)	125	130
Spaghetti, wholemeal (boiled)	125	141

BREAD

	Average portion (g)	Calories
Ciabatta, plain	50	135
Croissants	60	224
Crumpets	40	83
Focaccia	50	147
French Baguette	40	109
Garlic Bread	20	73
Hot Cross Buns	50	155
Muffins, English, white	68	152
Pitta Bread	75	191
Rolls		
Brown	48	113
White, crusty	50	131
White, soft	45	114
Wholemeal	48	117
Sliced		
Brown	36	83
Granary	36	92
White	40	94
Wholemeal	40	93
Soda Bread, brown	130	267
Tortilla, soft	160	451

CEREALS

	Average portion (g)	Calories
Bran Flakes	30	95
Bran Strands	40	104
Corn Flakes	30	108
Frosted Flakes	30	113
Fruit and Fibre	40	147
Hoops, Honey	30	111
Muesli	50	184
Oat Flakes	30	107
Porridge, with milk and water	160	133
Porridge, with water	160	78
Porridge, with whole milk	160	186
Puffed Wheat	20	64
Rice Pops	30	111
Wheat, shredded	45	150
Wheat, shredded, mini	45	154
Wholewheat Biscuits	38	134

JAMS AND SPREADS

	Average portion (g)	Calories
Honey	16	91
Jam	15	39
Lemon Curd	15	42
Marmalade	15	26
Meat Extract	8	14
Peanut Butter, crunchy	25	152
Peanut Butter, smooth	25	156
Yeast Extract	4	9

DIPS

	Average portion (g)	Calories
Guacamole	45	58
Hummus	30	56
Taramasalata	45	227
Tzatziki	45	30

COLD DRINKS AND JUICES

	Average portion (g)	Calories
Apple Juice	160	61
Carrot Juice	160	38
Cola	160	66
Cola, diet	160	Trace
Grapefruit Juice	160	53
Lemonade	160	35
Lemonade, diet	160	Trace
Orange Juice, fresh	160	53
Pineapple Juice	160	66
Pomegranate Juice	160	70

HOT DRINKS

	Average portion (g)	Calories
Cappuccino, with semi-skimmed milk	190	46
Coffee, with semi-skimmed milk	190	13
Coffee, with skimmed milk	190	8
Coffee, with whole milk	190	15
Hot Chocolate, with semi-skimmed milk	190	135
Hot Chocolate, with skimmed milk	190	112
Hot Chocolate, with whole milk	190	171
Latte, with semi-skimmed milk	190	60
Latte, with skimmed milk	190	33
Latte, with whole milk	190	85
Tea, black	190	Trace
Tea, Chinese	190	2
Tea, green	190	Trace
Tea, herbal	190	2
Tea, with semi-skimmed milk	190	13
Tea, with skimmed milk	190	8
Tea, with whole milk	190	15

Index

apples
apple and berry strudels 126
apple and yogurt muesli 43
spiced apple porridge 42
Asian steamed chicken salad 94
asparagus with smoked salmon 71
aubergines
spicy aubergine curry 83

bananas
bananas en papillote 124
prune and banana crunch 42
beans
herby lamb with butter
beans 117
lamb and flageolet bean
stew 118
squash with red bean sauce
84
beef
green peppercorn steak 112
lean lasagne 114
Russian meatballs 113
Thai beef and pepper
stir-fry 112
berries
apple and berry strudels 126
blueberry bran muffins 45
broccoli
Italian broccoli and
egg salad 63
brûlées
brûlée vanilla cheesecake 136
mango and passion fruit 135
bulgar wheat
tabbouleh 102

cakes
blueberry bran muffins 45
cranberry muffins 46
plum and ricotta almond
cake 139
calves liver with garlic mash 121
carnival chicken 88
celeriac
chicken with celeriac cakes 85
champagne granita 130
cheese see goats' cheese; quark;
ricotta cheese
cheesecake, brûlée vanilla 136
chicken
Asian steamed chicken
salad 94
blackened chicken skewers 86
carnival chicken 88
chicken and spinach curry 89
chicken with celeriac cakes 85
chicken with spring
vegetables 93
cranberry chicken stir-fry 92
grilled chicken salad 62

lemon and rosemary
chicken 87
lime and chilli chicken
kebabs 90
spiced chicken and mango
salad 61
Tandoori chicken 91
chickpeas
squid, chickpea and pepper
stew 106
chillies
chilli and coriander fish
parcel 104
chilli rice noodles 72
Chinese spiced citrus salad 127
chocolate orange soufflé 133
clams with chorizo and
pimentón 109
clementines
mango and clementine
sorbet 129
coconut
plaice with coconut crust 97
coconut milk
coconut and butternut soup 53
coconut and lime ice cream 132
coleslaw
lime and ginger prawn 74
pork skewers with 116
crab Malabar Hill 79
cranberries
cranberry chicken stir-fry 92
cranberry muffins 46
cranberry yogurt smoothie 40
Creole pineapple wedges 123
crêpes, mushroom 66
cucumber
tzatziki 81
curries
chicken and spinach 89
fish and tomato 105
pea, egg and tofu 82
spicy aubergine 83

dates
pistachio and date squares 47
duck
tea-infused duck with pak
choi 95

eggs
asparagus with smoked
salmon 71
butternut squash and ricotta
frittata 68
ham and tomato omelettes 49
Italian broccoli and egg
salad 63
Moroccan baked eggs 48
pea, egg and tofu curry 82
shiitake mushroom omelette 64

figs, honeyed 128
fish
aromatic tamarind fish
broth 101
asparagus with smoked
salmon 71
chilli and coriander fish
parcel 104
fish and tomato curry 105
griddled tuna with shallot
jus 97
grilled sardines with
tabbouleh 102
halibut with papaya
salsa 100
masala roast cod 98
plaice with coconut crust
97
red mullet with baked
tomatoes 99
seafood zarzuela 110
sesame-crusted salmon 103
fruit
fruity summer milkshake 40
maple-glazed granola 44
see also individual types of
fruit

ginger
ginger and parsnip soup 52
lime and ginger prawn
coleslaw 74
red pepper and ginger soup
50
goats' cheese
honeyed figs 128
lentil and goats' cheese
salad 58
granita, champagne 130
granola, maple-glazed 44

ham and tomato omelettes 49

ice cream
coconut and lime 132
Italian broccoli and egg salad 63

jellies, Pimm's 134

kebabs
lime and chilli chicken 90
prawn and mango 76

lamb
herby lamb with butter
beans 117
lamb and flageolet bean
stew 118
Turkish lamb and potato
stew 119
leek and tomato filo tarts 69

lemons
lemon and caper pork
tenderloin 115
lemon and rosemary
chicken 87
lemony scallop skewers 107
lentils
lentil and goats' cheese
salad 58
red lentil dhal with okra 70
limes
coconut and lime ice cream 132
lime and chilli chicken
kebabs 90
lime and ginger prawn
coleslaw 74

mangoes
mango and clementine
sorbet 129
mango and passion fruit
brûlées 135
mango and passion fruit
trifle 128
prawn and mango kebabs 76
spiced chicken and mango
salad 61
milkshake, fruity summer 40
Moroccan baked eggs 48
muesli, apple and yogurt 43
muffins
blueberry bran 45
cranberry 46
mushrooms
baked field mushrooms 65
hot and sour mushroom
soup 54
mushroom crêpes 66
shiitake mushroom omelette
64
mussels
aromatic steamed 108
seafood zarzuela 110

nectarines, orangey baked 122
noodles
fragrant soba noodle soup 56
Vietnamese-style noodle
salad 60

oats
maple-glazed granola 44
okra, red lentil dhal with 70
omelettes
ham and tomato 49
shiitake mushroom 64
oranges
brûlée vanilla cheesecake 136
Chinese spiced citrus salad 127
chocolate orange soufflé 133
orangey baked nectarines 122

...tta, tiger prawns with 77
panna cotta, passion fruit 137
parsnips
 ginger and parsnip soup 52
passion fruit
 mango and passion fruit
 brûlées 135
 mango and passion fruit
 trifle 128
 passion fruit panna cotta 137
pea, egg and tofu curry 82
peaches
 peach consommé with
 raspberries 125
peppers
 red pepper and ginger soup 50
 split pea and pepper patties 81
 squid, chickpea and pepper
 stew 106
 Thai beef and pepper
 stir-fry 112
Pimm's jellies 134
pineapple
 Creole pineapple wedges 123
piri piri prawns 75
pistachio and date squares 47
plum and ricotta almond cake 139
pork
 lemon and caper pork
 tenderloin 115
 pork skewers with coleslaw 116
porridge, spiced apple 42
potatoes
 calves liver with garlic
 mash 121
 Turkish lamb and potato
 stew 119

prawns
 hot and sour prawn soup 55
 lime and ginger prawn
 coleslaw 74
 piri piri prawns 75
 prawn and mango kebabs 76
 tiger prawns with pancetta 77
prune and banana crunch 42

quark
 brûlée vanilla cheesecake 136

ragout, turkey 96
ricotta cheese
 butternut squash and ricotta
 frittata 68
 plum and ricotta almond
 cake 139
roulade, strawberry 138
Russian meatballs 113

salads
 Asian steamed chicken 94
 grilled chicken 62
 Italian broccoli and egg 63
 lentil and goats' cheese 58
 lime and ginger prawn
 coleslaw 74
 spiced chicken and mango 61
 Vietnamese-style noodle 60
salsa, papaya 100
scallops
 lemony scallop skewers 107
smoothie, cranberry yogurt 40
sorbet, mango and clementine
 129
soufflé, chocolate orange 133

soups
 aromatic tamarind fish
 broth 101
 butternut and rosemary 57
 coconut and butternut 53
 fragrant soba noodle 56
 ginger and parsnip 52
 hot and sour mushroom 54
 hot and sour prawn 55
 quick and easy miso 53
 red pepper and ginger 50
spinach
 chicken and spinach curry 89
split pea and pepper patties 81
squashes
 butternut squash and ricotta
 frittata 68
 coconut and butternut soup
 53
 squash with red bean sauce 84
squid
 salt and pepper squid 78
 seafood zarzuela 110
 squid, chickpea and pepper
 stew 106
stews
 basil and tomato 67
 lamb and flageolet bean 118
 squid, chickpea and pepper 106
 Turkish lamb and potato 119
 zarzuela 110
stir-fries
 cranberry chicken 92
 Thai beef and pepper
 stir-fry 112
strawberries
 champagne granita 130

Pimm's jellies 134
 strawberry roulade 138

tabbouleh, grilled sardines
 with 102
Tandoori chicken 91
tarts, leek and tomato filo 69
Thai beef and pepper stir-fry 112
Thai dressed rolls 73
tofu
 pea, egg and tofu curry 82
tomatoes
 basil and tomato stew 67
 fish and tomato curry 105
 ham and tomato omelettes 49
 leek and tomato filo tarts 69
 red mullet with baked
 tomatoes 99
trifle, mango and passion fruit 12
turkey ragout 96
Turkish lamb and potato stew 11
tzatziki 81

veal with lemon 120
vegetables, chicken with
 spring 93
Vietnamese-style noodle salad 6

yogurt
 apple and yogurt muesli 43
 cranberry yogurt smoothie 40

Acknowledgements

PICTURE ACKNOWLEDGEMENTS

Getty Images/Blend Images/John Fedele 22; Mike Harrington 27; Photo by Ira Heuvelman-Dobrolyubova 18; Andersen Ross 17; J. Shepherd 19.

Octopus Publishing Group/Stephen Conroy 93, 94, 111, 131; Will Heap 4; Lis Parsons 1 right, 38, 41, 43, 45, 48, 49, 55, 56, 60, 68, 74, 80, 83, 89, 99, 103, 116, 122, 135, 137; Bill Reavell 121; Russell Sadur 20, 28; Gareth Sambidge 59, 126; William Shaw 46, 71, 77, 104; Simon Smith 1 left, 51, 54, 66, 69, 96, 113.

Thinkstock/Bananastock 29; George Doyle 11, 23; iStockphoto 9, 15, 21; Stockbyte 32; Wavebreak Media 7, 25, 31.

Publisher: Sarah Ford
Managing Editor: Clare Churly
Designer: Eoghan O'Brien
Layouts by Jeremy Tiltson
Picture Library Manager: Jennifer Veall
Senior Production Manager: Peter Hunt